PRAYER

✠

PRAYER

O. Hallesby

TRANSLATED BY

CLARENCE J. CARLSEN

FOREWORD BY

RICHARD J. FOSTER

✠

PRAYER

Scripture quotations are from the Holy Bible, King James Version.

Study guide by Dan Berka

Cover design by Cindy Cobb Olson

Interior design by James F. Brisson

Library of Congress Cataloging-in-Publication Data

Hallesby, Ole 1879-1961.
Prayer : updated version / by O. Hallesby.
p. cm.
Includes bibliographical references.
ISBN 0-8066-2700-X (acid-free paper)
1. Prayer. I. Title.
BV210.2.H34 1994
248.3'2—dc20 93-44780
CIP

The paper used in this publication meets the minimum requirements of American National Standard for Information Sciences—Permanence of Paper for Printed Library Materials, ANSI Z329.48-1984. ∞™

Manufactured in the U.S.A. AF 9-2700

CONTENTS

✠

FOREWORD

✠

We have come to the best of Norwegian Christian piety when we discover Ole Hallesby's *Prayer.* Instinctively we sense that here is someone who understands prayer. He understands its complexity and he understands its simplicity. Best of all, he helps us understand these things as well.

I like many things about this book. Let me comment upon four of them here.

First, more profoundly than most, Hallesby understands what prayer is and what it is not. He connects deeply with the essence of prayer when he says simply, "To pray is to let Jesus come into our hearts." In saying this he underscores the fact that *we* do not make prayer happen—that is God's business. Our task—our only task—is to make ourselves available for this glorious interactive communication between a finite spirit and the infinite Spirit of the universe. All of this is exceedingly good news, for as Hallesby notes, "The results of prayer are, therefore, not dependent upon the powers of the one who prays."

In another place he says, "Prayer is given and ordained for the purpose of glorifying God." This takes us beyond all those manipulative attempts to get God to give us something—which Hallesby calls a pagan rather than a Christian approach to prayer. Prayer is not using God to our own ends, nor is it making something happen. No, prayer is dependence, openness, trust, and listening love.

Second, I like Hallesby's ability to hold in creative tension the various paradoxes of prayer. He describes prayer as both a "resting place" and a "workshop"; as involving both utter dependence upon God and energetic wrestling with

God. In this regard he brings together a very unusual combination when he declares, "true prayer is a fruit of helplessness and faith." Seldom are these two ideas held together. We usually think of faith as active confidence, but Hallesby sees faith acting out of helplessness. In fact, he talks about helplessness a lot. Listen: "My helpless friend, your helplessness is the most powerful plea which rises up to the tender father-heart of God. . . . Helplessness is the real secret and the impelling power of prayer."

I am intrigued by his emphasis upon helplessness, because this is often how I actually experience prayer. It encourages me to learn that faith is not always some bold action; but rather at times it is a helpless stumbling and bumbling which, with all its weakness, nevertheless still turns to God. Such an experience of faith resonates well with the Gospel story of the father who out of sheer love for his son cries out to Jesus, "I believe, help my unbelief." Often this is the best we can do. It is enough.

Third, I am tantalized by a phrase Hallesby uses throughout the book: "the Spirit of prayer." He writes, "The one great secret of prayer is the Spirit of prayer." At another point he says, "All wrestling in prayer must bring us into harmony with the Spirit of prayer." It is not immediately clear what he means by the phrase. Sometimes it seems he is urging us into unity with the Holy Spirit, the author of all true prayer. At other times he appears to be calling us into an overall attitude and atmosphere of a prayerful spirit. Perhaps he means both.

Both are certainly needed in the work of prayer. At one point he speaks powerfully to both these ideas: "The real purpose of our wrestling in prayer is, therefore, to render us so impotent and helpless, not only in connection with our physical and spiritual needs, but, above all, our inability to pray, that our prayer really becomes a prayer for the Spirit of prayer."

This leads me to my fourth observation, namely, that this book itself breathes the spirit of prayer. It "smells Gospel" if you will. It is a book full of grace and mercy, jubilee and challenge. In it I sense Jesus inviting us to the adventure. And when all has been said and done, I can think of no greater commendation for a book on the topic of prayer.

Richard J. Foster

AUTHOR'S PREFACE

✠

I HAVE had more of a desire to write this book than possibly any other that I have written. And yet I have been more afraid of this one than of any other. It seems to me that it is very difficult to speak or write about prayer.

This book does not presume to be anything more than a presentation of a few simple rules for the benefit of souls who are fainting in prayer. It does not aim to give an exhaustive treatment of the great theme.

My one desire and prayer has been to preach the Gospel of prayer without setting aside any of the laws governing the prayer life.

O. Hallesby

BOOK ONE

What Prayer Is

"Behold, I stand at the door and knock: if any man hear my voice and open the door, I will come in to him, and will sup with him, and he with me."

—REVELATION 3:20.

I DOUBT that I know of a passage in the whole Bible which throws greater light upon prayer than this one does. It is, it seems to me, the key which opens the door into the holy and blessed realm of prayer.

To pray is to let Jesus come into our hearts.

This teaches us, in the first place, that it is not our prayer which moves the Lord Jesus. It is Jesus who moves us to pray. He knocks. Thereby He makes known His desire to come in to us. Our prayers are always a result of Jesus' knocking at our hearts' doors.

This throws new light upon the old prophetic passages: "Before they call, I will answer; and while they are yet speaking, I will hear" (Isaiah 65:24). Yea, verily, before we call, He graciously makes known to us what gift He has decided to impart to us. He knocks in order to move us by prayer to open the door and accept the gift which He has already appointed for us.

From time immemorial prayer has been spoken of as the breath of the soul. And the figure is an excellent one indeed.

The air which our body requires envelops us on every hand. The air of itself seeks to enter our bodies and, for this reason, exerts pressure upon us. It is well known that it is more difficult to hold one's breath than it is to breathe. We need but exercise our organs of respiration, and air will enter forthwith into our lungs and perform its life-giving function to the entire body.

The air which our souls need also envelops all of us at all times and on all sides. God is round about us in Christ on every hand, with His many-sided and all-sufficient grace. All we need to do is to open our hearts.

Prayer is the breath of the soul, the organ by which we receive Christ into our parched and withered hearts.

He says, "If any man open the door, I will come in to him."

Notice carefully every word here. It is not our prayer which draws Jesus into our hearts. Nor is it our prayer which moves Jesus to come in to us.

All He needs is access. He enters in of His own accord, because He desires to come in. And He enters in wherever He is not denied admittance.

As air enters in quietly when we breathe, and does its normal work in our lungs, so Jesus enters quietly into our hearts and does His blessed work there.

He calls it to "sup with us."

In Biblical language the common meal is symbolical of intimate and joyous fellowship. This affords a new glimpse into the nature of prayer, showing us that God has designed prayer as a means of intimate and joyous fellowship between God and humankind.

✠

Notice how graciously prayer has been designed.

To pray is nothing more involved than to let Jesus into our needs. To pray is to give Jesus permission to employ His powers in the alleviation of our distress. To pray is to let Jesus glorify His name in the midst of our needs.

The results of prayer are, therefore, not dependent upon the powers of the one who prays. Our intense will, our fervent emotions, or our clear comprehension of what we are praying for are not the reasons why our prayers will be heard and answered. Nay, God be praised, the results of prayer are not dependent upon these things!

To pray is nothing more involved than to open the door, giving Jesus access to our needs and permitting Him to exercise His own power in dealing with them.

He who gave us the privilege of prayer knows us very well. He knows our frame; He remembers that we are dust.

That is why He designed prayer in such a way that the most impotent can make use of it. For to pray is to open the door unto Jesus. And that requires no strength. It is only a question of our wills. Will we give Jesus access to our needs? That is the one great and fundamental question in connection with prayer.

When Israel had sinned against the Lord in the wilderness, He sent among them exceedingly fiery serpents. In their distress the people humbled themselves and cried to God for mercy. And the Lord had mercy upon His rebellious people. But He did not take away the serpents. What He did was to tell Moses to raise up a serpent of brass in the midst of the camp, that all might see it. And He ordained it so in His mercy that they who had been bitten by the serpents needed but to turn and look unto the serpent of brass, and they would be given the power which would heal them from the death-dealing poison of the serpents' bites.

This was indeed a gracious ordinance. By this all could be saved if they so willed.

If the Lord had ordained that those who had been bitten by the serpents must drag themselves over to the serpent of brass and touch it, most of them would never have been saved, because the poison took effect almost immediately, and those who had been poisoned were unable to walk more than a few steps. All that was required of them was to turn their heads, look unto the serpent of brass, and they would be healed!

Just so has the Lord in mercy ordained help also for the serpent-bitten Israel of the New Covenant: "And as Moses lifted up the serpent in the wilderness, even so must the Son of man be lifted up; that whosoever believeth may in him have eternal life" (John 3:14-15).

No matter in what distress we may be, distress of body or of soul, we need but look unto Him who is always near with that healing power which can immediately overcome the death-dealing poison of sin and its terrible consequences both to body and soul.

To pray is nothing more involved than to lift the eye of prayer unto the Savior who stands and knocks, yea knocks through our very need, in order to gain access to our distress, sup with us and glorify His name.

Let us think of patients who are ill with tuberculosis.

The physicians put them out in the sunlight and fresh air, both in summer and in winter. There they lie until a cure is gradually effected by the rays of the sun. The recovery of these patients is not dependent upon their thinking, in the sense of understanding the effect of the sun's rays or how these rays work. Neither does their recovery depend upon the feelings they experience during the rest cure.

Nor does it depend upon their wills in the sense of exerting themselves to will to become well.

On the contrary, the treatment is most successful if the patients lie very quietly and are passive, exerting neither their intellects nor their wills. It is the sun which effects the cure. All the patients need to do is to be in the sun.

Prayer is just as simple.

We are all saturated with the pernicious virus of sin; every one of us is a tubercular patient doomed to die! But "the sun of righteousness with healing in its wings has arisen." All that is required of us, if we desire to be healed both for time and for eternity, is to let the Son of righteousness reach us, and then to abide in the sunlight of His righteousness.

To pray is nothing more involved than to lie in the sunshine of His grace, to expose our distress of body and soul to those healing rays which can in a wonderful way counteract and render ineffective the bacteria of sin. To be a man or woman of prayer is to take this sun-cure, to give Jesus, with His wonder-working power, access to our distress night and day.

To be a Christian is in truth to have gained a place in the sun!

Permit me to use still another illustration to show how simple the Lord has made prayer.

The man sick of the palsy, mentioned in the second chapter of Mark, had some very good friends. They knew that Jesus could help him. So they carried him to the house where Jesus was. But they could not get in because of the multitude. Undaunted, they lifted the sick man to the roof, made a hole in it and lowered him to the very feet of Jesus.

There these good friends undoubtedly stood and waited for the authoritative word from Jesus by which their sick friend would immediately become well. But, strange enough, no such word was forthcoming from Jesus. Instead they heard these words spoken with authority: "Son, thy sins are forgiven!"

Another prayer had been crying louder to Jesus. It was the sick man's plea for the forgiveness of sins. And yet he had not spoken one word to Jesus. He was lying quietly on his bed. It is easy for me to think that he lay there looking to Jesus, only looking to Jesus.

And Jesus heard the unuttered prayer for the forgiveness of sins which arose from the sick man's heart. And He answered this prayer first. Afterward He answered the other prayer also and restored the man to physical health.

✠

Helplessness.

This helps us to get a little deeper insight into the secret of prayer.

Prayer is something deeper than words. It is present in the soul before it has been formulated in words. And it abides in the soul after the last words of prayer have passed over our lips.

Prayer is an attitude of our hearts, an attitude of mind. Prayer is a definite attitude of our hearts toward God, an attitude which He in heaven immediately recognizes as prayer, as an appeal to His heart. Whether it takes the form of words or not, does not mean anything to God, only to ourselves.

What is this spiritual condition? What is that attitude of heart which God recognizes as prayer? I would mention two things.

In the first place, helplessness.

This is unquestionably the first and the surest indication of a praying heart. As far as I can see, prayer has been ordained only for the helpless. It is the last resort of the helpless. Indeed, the very last way out. We try everything before we finally resort to prayer.

This is not only true of us before our conversion. Prayer is our last resort also throughout our whole Christian life. I know very well that we offer many and beautiful prayers, both privately and publicly, without helplessness as the impelling power. But I am not at all positive that this is prayer.

Prayer and helplessness are inseparable. Only those who are helpless can truly pray.

Listen to this, you who are often so helpless that you do not know what to do. At times you do not even know how to pray. Your mind seems full of sin and impurity. Your mind is preoccupied with what the Bible calls the world. God and eternal and holy things seem so distant and foreign to you that you feel that you add sin to sin by desiring to approach God in such a state of mind. Now and then you must ask yourself the question, "Do I really desire to be set free from the lukewarmness of my heart and my worldly life? Is not my Christian life always lukewarm and half-hearted for the simple reason that deep down in my heart I desire it that way?"

Thus honest souls struggle against the dishonesty of their own being. They feel themselves so helplessly lost that their prayers freeze on their very lips.

Listen, my friend! Your helplessness is your best prayer. It calls from your heart to the heart of God with greater effect than all your uttered pleas. He hears it from the very moment that you are seized with helplessness, and He becomes actively engaged at once in hearing and answering the prayer of your helplessness. He hears today as He heard the helpless and wordless prayer of the man sick with the palsy.

If you are a mother, you will understand very readily this phase of prayer.

Your infant children cannot formulate in words a single petition to you. Yet the little ones pray the best way they know how. All they can do is cry, but you understand very well their pleading.

Moreover, the little ones need not even cry. All YOU need to do is to see them in all their helpless dependence upon you, and a prayer touches your mother-heart, a prayer which is stronger than the loudest cry.

He who is the Father of all that is called mother and all that is called child in heaven and on earth deals with us in the same way. Our helplessness is one continuous appeal to His father-heart. He is forever occupied with hearing this prayer of ours and satisfying all our needs. Night and day He is active in so doing, although we as a rule do not even notice it, not to speak of thanking Him for it.

If you are a mother, you will understand this, too, better than the rest of us. You care for your little ones night and day, even though they do not understand what you are doing, sacrificing and suffering for them. They do not thank you, and often they are even contrary, causing you not a little difficulty. But you do not let that hinder you. You hear and answer incessantly the prayer which their helplessness sends up to your mother-heart.

Such is God.

Only that He does perfectly what human love can only do imperfectly. As a true mother dedicates her life to the care of her children, so the eternal God in His infinite mercy has dedicated Himself eternally to the care of His frail and erring children.

Thus God deals with us all.

Also with you, my unconverted reader. Most likely you think that God does not love you. At times you even think that He pays no attention to you whatsoever. At other times again you feel as though God is pursuing you with vengeance and retaliation, as though He were seeking to upset your plans and destroy your happiness.

Listen, and I will tell you what God is like: "He maketh his sun to rise on the evil and on the good, and sendeth rain on the just and on the unjust" (Matthew 5:45). Christ spent His last strength and His last moments in prayer for His enemies. "Father, forgive them; for they know not what they do" (Luke 23:34). When Jesus returned to Jerusalem for the last time and had no further means of saving the ungodly and rebellious city, He stood on the Mount of Olives and wept for the city. His prophetic eye saw the terrible doom which would befall the city and from which there was no escape.

Such is God.

He loves His enemies. When He sees the distress of the ungodly, their empty joys and their real sorrows, their disappointments, their sufferings and their anxieties as they are irresistibly swept along by the stream of time toward the everlasting anguish of hell, their distress and helplessness cry to His heart. And He hears their cry and stoops down to helpless mortals in order to help them.

The unconverted accepts His help when it pertains to temporal things. But as soon as God offers spiritual help the helpless person turns away and often flees from God in great terror. Such a person refuses to be converted!

✠

Prayer is for the helpless.

Behold sinners who no longer flee from God. They stand in the light of heaven. More or less gradually they begin to see their former sins, the boundless depths of impurity in their heart, their impenitent coolness, indifference and rebelliousness toward God, their dislike of the Bible and of prayer and the permanent desire of their weak will towards sin.

What do they do now?

Like everybody else they cry in their distress to God.

They cry more or less intensely, more or less often, more or less regularly. But they receive no answer from God. They feel that they are forsaken, that they are like someone being driven along on an upturned keel out on the open, raging sea. They cry with all their strength. They cannot stop even though not a soul can hear them.

Then these helpless souls say to themselves, "God does not answer me because I do not pray right. Can my prayers really be called prayers? Are they anything but words, empty words? Do they reach higher than the roof? If I do not put more holy zeal and more decided determination into my prayers, they will not be prayers which God can hear."

My helpless friend, your helplessness is the most powerful plea which rises up to the tender father-heart of God. He has heard your prayer from the very first moment that you honestly cried to Him in your need, and night and day He inclines His ear toward earth in order to ascertain if there are any helpless mortals turning to Him in their distress.

Now listen again. It is not your prayer which moves God to save you. On the contrary, your prayer is a result of the fact that Jesus has knocked at your heart's door and told you that He desires to gain access to your needs. You think that everything is closed to you because you cannot pray. My friend, your helplessness is the very essence of prayer.

To pray is to open the door unto Jesus and admit Him into your distress. Your helplessness is the very thing which opens wide the door unto Him and gives Him access to all your needs.

"But why doesn't He answer me?" you ask perplexed.

He has answered your prayer.

He has entered into your life, through the door which you in your helplessness have opened for Him. He is already dwelling in your heart. He is doing the good work within you.

As yet you have not really understood His answer. But in this respect you are like all the rest of us who pray. We pray, and our prayers are answered; but we do not see the answer immediately, often not until a long time afterward.

You have imagined that you would receive an answer from God according to your own thinking, and that you would receive either peace, assurance or joy in your soul. Not receiving these things, you thought that God had not answered you. Jesus has many things to tell us and much to accomplish within us which we do not understand at the time. We are impatient and think that He ought to do something else for us or say something else to us than what He does, just as Peter did when Jesus washed the disciples' feet (John 13:1-10). But Jesus does not permit Himself to be disturbed by our impatience. He proceeds calmly, saying, "What I do thou knowest not now; but thou shalt understand hereafter" (John 13:7).

Be not anxious because of your helplessness. Above all, do not let it prevent you from praying. Helplessness is the real secret and the impelling power of prayer. You should therefore rather try to thank God for the feeling of helplessness which He has given you. It is one of the greatest gifts which God can impart to us. For it is only when we are helpless that we open our hearts to Jesus and let Him help us in our distress, according to His grace and mercy.

From the heavenly perspective many things look different than they do here on earth. I think that our prayers, too, look different when viewed from above.

There is, for instance, the prayer meeting. One after another prays. First they pray who are accustomed to pray aloud in the presence of others. They pray well, and their prayers edify. When they say, Amen, everybody acquiesces quietly in the fact that it was a good prayer. But at the same prayer meeting there may also be another believing soul who would like very much to lift his or her voice in prayer at the meeting. This individual feels a greater need, perhaps, than any of the others. However, being not accustomed to it, the person does not succeed very well in the effort. Thoughts become disconnected, and the speaker stumbles. Finally the person becomes bewildered and even forgets to say, Amen. After the meeting the speaker is so downcast because of the prayer offered and because of the condition of his or her heart that he or she scarcely dares to look anyone in the face.

But I know that a new song of praise has already been sung by the saints in glory, rejoicing because they have heard someone pray to God who in his or her helplessness did not know what else to do. Such prayers make an impression in heaven.

✠

Let me say one more word about helplessness in prayer.

It can be experienced in various ways. Especially may it result in widely varying reactions in our emotional life. As a rule we will feel our helplessness most, it will make the deepest impression upon our emotional life, in the beginning of our Christian life.

During the time when the Lord is making us humble of spirit and contrite of heart (Isaiah 57:15), when He is crushing our self-conceit and self-sufficiency, our emotional life will no doubt be stirred most profoundly. Not because it is all so new and strange, but mostly because it is so incomprehensible.

God is such that we cannot fully understand Him. He is so great that none of His creatures can comprehend Him completely. No one can meet God without discovering that he or she can not understand God fully.

As mentioned above, it does not take long before an awakened sinner realizes that some of God's ways are past finding out. "Why do I not receive peace, assurance and joy? Why does not God help me out of the distress which I can no longer endure? Why does He let me sink into eternal perdition when He sees how earnestly I desire to be saved? Why does He not answer with a single word any of the distressing cries which arise from my soul?"

We can endure a great many things with a calm mind if we can see the reason for, or the purpose of, our suffering. It is that which we cannot understand and which therefore seems meaningless that irritates us and makes us rebellious more than anything else. For that reason no aspect of God becomes a stumblingblock to us more easily than His inscrutability. It reminds us of the poignant words of Jesus, "Blessed are they, whosoever shall find no occasion of stumbling in me" (Matthew 11:6).

For this reason no aspect of God breaks down our self-conceit and our self-sufficiency more quickly than this. For the first time we come to a point where we do not know what to do. We are unable to go back to our former life, and we cannot find the way to God. We have not learned as yet to surrender to a God whose ways are past finding out. As a result our whole being is in a state of rebelliousness. That which is incomprehensible always fills us with paralyzing fear.

All of us who continue in this fear and do not flee from God or our own conscience, and who tarry in the presence of the inscrutable God, experience a miracle, God breaks down our self-conceit and self-sufficiency. Without knowing how, we helpless souls are drawn into the fellowship of our incomprehensible God. God Himself in Christ enables us to humble ourselves beneath the inscrutability of God, to endure it, and to rely upon and rest in the God whose way we cannot fully understand.

Thereby a thing of decisive importance has taken place in the lives of us sinners.

We have become reconciled not only to the inscrutability of God but also to our own helplessness. While up to this time this has put our whole being into a state of rebelliousness and anxiety, now we have experienced the fact that helplessness is a sinner's proper plea in the presence of God.

Not by reflection, but by the certainty of experience, we know now that an infant is no more helpless in its relation to its mother than we are in our relation to God. At all points we are equally helpless: whether it be in connection with the forgiveness of sins, the conquest of sin, the new life in our souls, growth in grace or faithfulness in our daily life with God and other people.

Our helplessness now becomes a new factor in our prayer life.

Before, our helplessness was the storm center of our prayer life, either driving us to supplicatory cries of distress, or stopping our mouths so effectively that we could not find a single word with which to give utterance to our needs.

Our helplessness has now become the quiet, sustaining power of our prayer life. A humble and contrite heart knows that it can merit nothing before God, and that all that is necessary is to be reconciled to one's helplessness and let our holy and almighty God care for us, just as an infant surrenders itself to its mother's care.

Prayer therefore consists simply in telling God day by day in what ways we feel that we are helpless. We are moved to pray every time the Spirit of God, which is the spirit of prayer, emphasizes anew to us our helplessness, and we realize how impotent we are by nature to believe, to love, to hope, to serve, to sacrifice, to suffer, to read the Bible, to pray and to struggle against our sinful desires.

It often happens that we slip out of this blessed attitude of helplessness before God. Our former self-conceit and self-sufficiency reassert themselves. The result is that we fail again to grasp the meaning of helplessness. Once more it fills us with anxiety and perplexity. Everything becomes snarled again. We are not certain of the forgiveness of sins. The peace of God disappears from our lives. Worldliness, slothfulness and lack of spiritual interest begin to choke our spiritual lives. Sin gains the victory again in our daily lives, and an unwilling spirit works its way into the service we render toward God.

This continues until God again can make us humble and contrite of heart and we again become reconciled to being helpless sinners, who can do nothing but this one thing: to permit the infinite God to have mercy on us, to love us and care for us. Then our helplessness reestablishes us in our right relationship both to God and to others. Above all it restores us to the right attitude in prayer.

Helplessness in prayer resembles in a striking way the condition of a person who is lame or sick of the palsy. At first it is painful, almost unbearable, to be so helpless that we cannot hold a spoon to our mouth or chase a fly from our face. It is easy to understand why persons thus afflicted cannot experience this without strong inner revulsion and protest, at the same time as they put forth the most intense efforts to use their limbs as before.

But notice these same persons after they have become resigned to their illness and reconciled to their helplessness. They are just as helpless as they were before, but their helplessness no longer causes them any pain or anxiety. It has become a part of them and has set its stamp upon all their movements and all their attitudes.

Such persons must be helped in everything. It feels very humiliating. Notice, too, how this humiliation has set its stamp upon them. When they quietly and humbly ask for help, they do so as though they were apologizing for doing so. Notice, too, how grateful they are for the least bit of assistance that they receive.

All their thinking and all their planning have been conditioned by their helplessness. They are, of course, dependent in all things upon those who care for them. We notice, too, that this feeling of dependence develops into a peculiar bond of sympathy between the afflicted person and the caretaker, the strongest bond by which human beings can become attached to one another.

Thus our helplessness should make us attached to God and make us more strongly dependent upon Him than words can describe. Recall to mind the words of Jesus, "Without me ye can do nothing" (John 15:5). In one single line He tells us here what it takes us a whole lifetime to learn, and even when we reach the portals of death we have not learned it fully.

I never grow weary of emphasizing our helplessness, for it is the decisive factor not only in our prayer life, but in our whole relationship to God. As long as we are conscious of our helplessness we will not be overtaken by any difficulty, disturbed by any distress or frightened by any hindrance. We will expect nothing of ourselves and therefore bring all our difficulties and hindrances to God in prayer. And this means to open the door unto Him and to give God the opportunity to help us in our helplessness by means of the miraculous powers which are at His disposal.

✠

Faith.

I come now to another aspect of that attitude which constitutes the essence of prayer, that condition of the heart which God recognizes as prayer rising to Him from earth, whether it is uttered or not.

It is written, "Without faith it is impossible to be well-pleasing unto him" (Hebrews 11:6). Without faith there can be no prayer, no matter how great our helplessness may be. Helplessness united with faith produces prayer. Without faith our helplessness would be only a vain cry of distress in the night.

I need but mention faith, and every man and woman of prayer will know that we are touching upon one of the aspects of prayer life about which we are most sensitive.

The Bible contains many pointed passages about praying in faith if we expect to be heard.

"If ye have faith, and doubt not, ye shall not only do what is done to the fig tree, but even if ye shall say unto this mountain, Be thou taken up and cast into the sea, it shall be done. And all things, whatsoever ye shall ask in prayer, believing, ye shall receive" (Matthew 21:21-22).

"Said I not unto thee, that, if thou believedst, thou shouldest see the glory of God?" (John 11:40).

"As thou hast believed, so be it done unto thee" (Matthew 8:13).

"But let him ask in faith, nothing doubting: for he that doubteth is like the surge of the sea driven by the wind and tossed. For let not that man think that he shall receive anything of the Lord; a doubleminded man, unstable in all his ways" (James 1:6-8).

These words have sent many a poor man and woman of prayer down into the dust of despair and rendered them so completely helpless that they have felt it impossible to pray. It is all so self-evident. Those who would pray to God must believe in God. It is blasphemy toward God to turn to Him in prayer and not believe in answer to prayer.

Honest souls who examine themselves in the light of the Scriptures soon find that faith is just what seems lacking in their prayers. It says that they should ask in faith, nothing doubting. They do just the opposite. They doubt before they pray, while they pray and after they have prayed. They are just like the surge of the sea; they are driven and tossed to and fro by the winds of doubt. They are the very ones whom Scripture depicts: "a double-minded man, unstable in all his ways."

They are in distress; they are helpless; and they pray. But they do not receive what they pray for, even though they pray fervently and frequently and cry to God in their distress, on their own behalf as well as on behalf of their loved ones. After such a prayer the secret hope surges through their souls: Perhaps God will hear me this time? They wait intently for an answer. But, alas, no change occurs.

They feel that God has passed judgment upon their prayer. God cannot hear them because they do not pray in faith. They pray, doubting. Alas, how doubt bores its way into every prayer! It makes them anxious and afraid of prayer, afraid of sinning against God by the very act of praying.

My doubting friend, your case is not as bad as you think it is.

You have more faith than you think you have. You have faith enough to pray; you have faith enough to believe that you will be heard. Faith is a strange thing; it often conceals itself in such a way that we can neither see nor find it. Nevertheless, it is there; and it manifests itself by definite and unmistakable signs. Let us examine these briefly.

The essence of faith is to come to Christ.

This is the first and the last and the surest indication that faith is still alive. A sinner has nothing but sin and distress. The Spirit of God has made that clear to the sinner. And faith manifests itself clearly and plainly when sinners, instead of fleeing from God and their own responsibility, as they did before, come into the presence of Christ with all their sin and all their distress. The sinner who does this believes.

It is written, "Him that cometh to me I will in no wise cast out" (John 6:37). "If we confess our sins, he is faithful and righteous to forgive us our sins, and to cleanse us from all unrighteousness" (1 John 1:9).

That was just what those people did who came to Christ and heard from Him these words before they departed, "Thy faith hath saved thee." All they did was to come to Jesus and plead their distress before Him, whether it was physical or spiritual or both.

Notice the simple, but unmistakable, mark of a living faith.

Such a faith as this sees its own need, acknowledges its own helplessness, goes to Jesus, tells Him just how bad things are and leaves everything with Him.

You and I can now tell how much faith we need in order to pray. We have faith enough when we in our helplessness turn to Jesus.

This shows us clearly that true prayer is a fruit of helplessness and faith. Helplessness becomes prayer the moment that you go to Jesus and speak candidly and confidently with him about your needs. This is to believe.

The reason that more faith than this is not necessary in order to pray lies in the very nature of prayer.

We have seen above that prayer is nothing more involved than to open the door when Jesus knocks and give Him access to our distress and helplessness with all His miracle-working powers.

It is not intended that our faith should help Jesus to fulfill our supplications. He does not need any help; all he needs is access. Neither is it intended that our faith should draw Jesus into our distress, or make Him interested in us, or solicitous on our behalf. He has long since cared for us. And He Himself would like to gain access to our distress in order to help us. But He can not gain admittance until we "open the door," that is, until we in prayer give Him an opportunity to intervene.

✠

You have looked upon that state of doubt and inner uncertainty, in which you so often have gone into and returned from the hour of prayer, as unbelief. This is due to confused thinking, which, alas, is very common, but none the less dangerous to our prayer life.

Unbelief is something very different from doubt. Unbelief is an attribute of the will and consists in the refusal to believe, that is, refusal to see one's own need, acknowledge one's helplessness, go to Jesus and speak candidly and confidently with Him about one's sin and distress.

Doubt, on the other hand, is anguish, a pain, a weakness, which at times affects our faith. We could therefore call it faith-distress, faith-anguish, faith-suffering, faith-tribulation.

Such faith-illness can be more or less painful and more or less protracted, like all other ailments. But if we can begin to look upon it as suffering which has been laid upon us, it will lose its sting of distress and confusion.

All suffering which is laid upon us should work together for our good. So also faith-suffering. It is not as dangerous as we feel that it is. It is not harmful to faith nor to prayer. It does serve to render us helpless. And, as we have seen above, helplessness is, psychologically, the sustaining and impelling power of prayer. Nothing so furthers our prayer life as the feeling of our own helplessness.

These thoughts seem, however, to conflict with the Scripture passages cited above. They stated categorically that he who prays, doubting, cannot expect to be heard.

But these passages must not be torn out of their context. We must compare them with other passages of the Scriptures bearing on the same thought. Special mention must be made of the characteristic little account in Mark 9:14-30. While Jesus and three of His twelve disciples were experiencing the Transfiguration on the mountain top, a man had brought his boy, possessed with demons, to the other disciples; but they were not able to cast out the evil spirit. When Jesus came, the father hastened to bring the child to Him.

In answer to Jesus' question, the father told Him how long the child had been thus afflicted and how terrible his suffering had been. Then he added in distress, "If thou canst do anything, have compassion on us, and help us." To which Jesus answered, "If thou canst believe! All things are possible to him that believeth." The man seemed to sense the seriousness of Jesus' words and exclaimed in distress, "I believe; help Thou mine unbelief!"

Here we have a typical example of doubting faith. Doubt, in this instance, and as is usually the case, follows two trends, one with reference to God and one with reference to faith. The man expresses exactly what he feels: "If thou canst do anything, have compassion on us and help us!" He is really not fully certain that Jesus can help him.

When Jesus had met his skepticism on this score by his incisive words about faith, "If thou canst believe! All things are possible to him that believeth," the man gave way completely. He felt the truth of Jesus' words, but he felt also that his faith was failing him. At that moment everything was at stake. But he knew not what else to do but to tell just exactly how faith and doubt were struggling for mastery in his soul. So he says, "I believe; help Thou mine unbelief!"

The characteristic thing to notice here is that he uses the expression unbelief. He himself condemns his doubt as unbelief. That is what sincere faith always does; it judges itself strictly and unmercifully.

But we should notice what judgment Jesus passed upon this doubting, unstable, shaky condition. In His eyes this was faith. This is clearly evident from the fact that Jesus healed the boy. Had the father's doubt actually been unbelief, Jesus would not have been able to heal him. This is clear from verse twenty-three. And this is stated with exceptional clearness in Mark 6:5-6: "And he could there do no mighty work. . . . And he marvelled because of their unbelief."

Here we see how weak, unstable and doubting faith can be.

Notice how faith at the moment of prayer condemned itself as unbelief. And yet faith was there.

It was there in sufficient degree to enable Jesus to perform one of His greatest miracles. The disciples had tried to heal the boy, but had failed.

What is the reason that such a weak, unstable and doubting faith could be heard and answered? Because it was characterized by the essence of living faith: it went to Jesus. It pleaded its distress before Him. It complained of its faith-distress by telling Jesus how full of doubt this faith was.

✠

The insight we have now gained into the nature of prayer and faith will undoubtedly simplify our prayer life and make it easier.

In the first place, it has become clear to us that the answer to prayer is not dependent upon our emotions or our thoughts before, during or after prayer. The illustration about the afflicted father in Mark 9 has shown us that plainly. His emotions were less than nothing to build upon both before, during and after his prayer. Everything seemed hopeless. The disciples had tried to heal his son, but had not succeeded. Then Jesus came. He insisted strongly on faith. When the poor father cried out in his distress, "I believe; help my unbelief," I wonder if he did not feel that every avenue was closed?

And his thoughts gave him no more encouragement than his feelings. He has told us some of the things he was thinking about. "If thou canst do anything?" He was not at all certain whether the Lord could succeed any better than the disciples. And when he understood from Jesus' words that it depended somewhat upon him, too, upon his faith, he despaired still more. He felt as though he were swinging to and fro between faith and unbelief.

This is something for us to think about, we who have exactly the same experiences when we pray. We vacillate between doubt and faith. We are not certain whether we are praying right, whether we are praying according to the will of God, or not. And even if we feel certain that what we are praying for is according to the will of God, there is frequently so little earnestness and sincerity in our prayer that we, for that reason, doubt that we will be heard. We feel that it is almost blasphemy toward God to pray in such a state of mind.

At such a time it is blessed to know that we have faith enough when we bring our needs to Jesus and leave them with Him. And though there be much doubt and but little faith in our hearts, we can do as the father did who came to Jesus. We can begin by telling Him about our doubts and our weak faith. This makes it easier for us, and we can pray more confidently.

I need not exert myself and try to force myself to believe, or try to chase doubt out of my heart. Both are equally useless. It begins to dawn on me that I can bring everything to Jesus, no matter how difficult it is; and I need not be frightened away by my doubts or my weak faith, but only tell Jesus how weak my faith is. I have let Jesus into my heart. And He will fulfill my heart's desire.

BOOK TWO

Difficulties in Prayer

TO PRAY is to open our hearts to Jesus. And Jesus is all that we sinners need both for time and eternity. He "was made unto us wisdom from God, and righteousness and sanctification, and redemption" (1 Corinthians 1:30). This gives us the Biblical view of the purpose of prayer, its place and significance in the divine dispensation of salvation.

Jesus said once, "Apart from me ye can do nothing" (John 15:5). He knew how literally true these words are, how entirely helpless we are without Him. But at the same time He said, "Ask, and it shall be given you." All that you need and more besides.

He never grew tired of inviting, prompting, encouraging, exhorting, even commanding us to pray. The many and various admonitions to prayer in the Bible shed remarkable light upon prayer. They show us that prayer is the heart-throb in the life of a saved person.

Permit me to cite a few of the gracious admonitions to prayer which the Lord has given us:

"Ask, and it shall be given you; seek, and ye shall find; knock, and it shall be opened unto you; for everyone that asketh receiveth; and he that seeketh findeth; and to him that knocketh it shall be opened. Or what man is there of you, who, if his son shall ask him for a loaf, will give him a stone; or if he shall ask for a fish will give him a serpent? If ye then, being evil, know how to give good gifts unto your children, how much more shall your Father who is in heaven give good things to them that ask him?" (Matthew 7:7-11).

"If ye abide in me, and my words abide in you, ask whatsoever ye will, and it shall be done unto you" (John 15:7).

"Be careful for nothing; but in everything by prayer and supplication with thanksgiving let your requests be made known unto God" (Philippians 4:6).

These three passages from Scripture alone, it appears to me, should be sufficient to show what Jesus meant prayer to be.

If I were to give expression to this meaning in my own words, I would put it about as follows:

Jesus comes to sinners, awakens them from their sleep in sin, converts them, forgives their sins and makes them His children. Then He takes the weak hand of the sinner and places it in His own strong, nail-pierced hand and says: "Come now, I am going with you all the way and will bring you safe home to heaven. If you ever get into trouble or difficulty, just tell me about it. I will give you, without reproach, everything you need, and more besides, day by day, as long as you live."

My friend, do you not also think that that is what Jesus really meant when He gave us prayer?

And that is the way we should make use of it. That is the way He desires to answer our prayer, graciously and abundantly. Prayer should be the means by which I, at all times, receive all that I need, and, for this reason, be my daily refuge, my daily consolation, my daily joy, my source of rich and inexhaustible joy in life.

From this it is very apparent also that children of God can grieve Jesus in no worse way than to neglect prayer. For by so doing they sever the connection between themselves and the Savior, and their inner life is doomed to be withered and crippled, as is the case with most of us. Many neglect prayer to such an extent that their spiritual life gradually dies out.

I seem to hear some of the bitter sorrow which proceeds from the heart of God when He is compelled to say to us, "Ye have not, because ye ask not" (James 4:2).

He has all that we need, and there is nothing that He would rather do than impart to us His gifts. But we do not ask. We do not have time, we say. Or we forget to pray. The result is that we go about at home and in the assembly of believers like spiritual cripples or dwarfs, spiritually starved and emaciated, with scarcely enough strength to stand on our own feet, not to speak of fighting against sin and serving the Lord.

I have sinned a great deal against my merciful heavenly Father since I was converted, and I have grieved Him a great deal during the twenty-five years that I have lived with Him. But the greatest sin that I have committed since my conversion, the way in which I have grieved my Lord the most, is in connection with prayer, my neglect of prayer. This neglect is the cause of my many other sins of omission as well as of commission.

The countless opportunities for prayer which I have failed to make use of, the many answers to prayer which God would have given me if I only had prayed, accuse me more and more violently the more I become acquainted with the holy realm of prayer.

✠

Why do most of us fail so miserably in prayer?

I have pondered this question nearly ever since I, by the grace of God, began to pray.

I think we will all admit, both to ourselves and to others, without any question, that to pray is difficult for all of us. The difficulty lies in the very act of praying. To pray, really to pray, is what is difficult for us. It feels like too much of an effort.

That natural persons feel that prayer is an effort is not strange in the least. They "receive not the things of the Spirit of God: for they are foolishness unto [them]" (1 Corinthians 2:14). "The mind of the flesh is enmity against God" (Romans 8:7).

Natural persons may, of course, feel a desire to pray at times. They may feel a desire to pray when they are in danger, for instance, or when they are in a religious frame of mind. But they can never become reconciled to daily and regular prayer. They feel that it is unreasonable on the part of God to be so particular about this matter of praying.

They give many reasons why they do not pray quite as many prayers as most pastors and preachers demand of them. They say to themselves: "The Lord certainly does not expect people who are well and strong and able to work to spend so much valuable time in prayer. Especially in these modern times when everybody is so busy."

Natural persons look upon prayer as a burdensome task. Most unspiritual people never assume this burden. Some do, however, and pray to God a little each day. But they feel that it is a heavy requirement, and they do so only because they think that our Lord is strict in regard to this and insists that it be done.

That this is the natural person's view of prayer does not surprise us.

It cannot help but surprise us, however, when we find that this view is prevalent also among believing Christians, at least among many of us.

At conversion we were led into a life of earnest, diligent prayer. Our seasons of prayer were the happiest time of the day. But after a longer or a shorter period of time, we began to encounter difficulties in our prayer life. Prayer became a burden, an effort. As honest souls we clung diligently and faithfully to prayer but often we had to compel ourselves to enter into our secret chambers. Prayer, which was once the free, happy, grateful communion of a redeemed soul with God, had begun to become a matter of duty, which we performed more or less punctiliously according to our character and the willpower we had.

The more of an effort prayer becomes, the more easily it is neglected. Results which are fatal to spiritual life follow, not immediately, but no less certainly. First, our minds become worldly, and we feel more and more alienated from God, and therefore have less and less about which to speak with Him. Then we develop an unwilling spirit, which always finds pretexts for not praying and excuses for having neglected prayer.

Our inner life begins to weaken. The pain of living in sin is not felt as keenly as before, because sin is no longer honestly confessed before God. As a result of this, again, our spiritual vision becomes blurred, and we can no longer distinguish clearly between that which is sin and that which is not. From now on we resist sin in essentially the same way as worldly people do. They struggle against those sins only which are exceedingly dangerous from the standpoint of their consequences.

But such people have no desire to lose their reputation as Christians. For this reason they try to hide the worldliness of their minds as long as possible. In conversation, as well as in the prayer meeting, they are tempted to use language which is not in harmony with their inner selves. Empty words and affectation now seek to strangle what little prayer life is left in their hearts.

All this and a great deal more is the result of an impaired prayer life. And this is just what has taken place in the lives of many believers.

✠

These sad experiences in connection with prayer, which I have had together with many others, have given me a great deal to reflect upon. At this point I would like to call attention to a few of these thoughts. I have asked myself if most of our difficulties in connection with prayer are not due to the fact that we do not pray right. Prayer is a fine, delicate instrument. To use it right is a great art, a holy art. There is perhaps no greater art than the art of prayer.

The other fine arts require a great deal of native ability, much knowledge and a great deal of money to cover the cost of a long and expensive period of training. Fortunately, such is not the case with the art of prayer. It requires neither great native ability, nor much knowledge, nor money. The least gifted, the uneducated and the poor can cultivate the holy art of prayer.

However, certain requirements must also be met if the art of prayer is to be acquired. In the main they are two: practice and perseverance. Without practice no Christian will become a real man or woman of prayer. And practice cannot be attained without perseverance.

The painful and disappointing experiences in connection with prayer which I have mentioned in the preceding are undoubtedly necessary for most of us; at least, they are unavoidable steps in the acquisition of that personal experience with prayer which we must gain for ourselves. They are a part of that practice which constitutes the prerequisite of a more fully developed life of prayer.

For that reason I do not think that we should look upon these painful experiences too pessimistically. Surely they are more profitable than we think at the time we are going through the anguish connected with them.

But if they are to be of any benefit to us, we must, in the first place, be truthful and not begin to practice deception, that is, excuse and defend our slovenly prayer life. We must admit our weakness in prayer, admit that we are face to face with a problem which cannot be solved by our own efforts.

To move in prayer as though one were in one's element, to pray daily with a willing spirit, with joy, with gratitude and with adoration is something which is far beyond our human capacities and abilities. A miracle of God is necessary every day for this. This miracle consists in receiving the Spirit of prayer.

The Spirit of prayer can teach us to pray. Through the Word and the daily exercise of prayer, He gives us the practice and the divine insight into the prayer life and its laws which we need in order to make us real men and women of prayer.

Little by little He convinces us from the Word of the mistakes we have made in praying. He shows us that our prayer life has become a strenuous effort because of the mistakes we have made in prayer. Then He shows us what the real meaning of prayer is and how we should pray. Little by little we acquire the right practice.

The same is true here as in acquiring proficiency in the use of any instrumentality. It is hard to use as long as we use it wrongly. And its effectiveness is correspondingly low. I can imagine someone taking hold of a shovel and beginning to use it as best he or she knows how, but upside down.

After working a while I can imagine hearing the person say, "It is hard work to use a shovel, and I cannot accomplish a great deal with it either."

We would be glad to be able to take the shovel into our own hands and show our friend how it should be used. After trying again for a while, he or she will exclaim, "How easy it is to use a shovel, and how much one can do with it!"

All of life has its own laws. Where these laws are followed, life is sound and strong, easily lived and bears an abundance of fruit.

The prayer life, too, has its laws. If we break these laws, if we pray contrary to the very idea and essence of what prayer is, our prayer life will be burdensome and fruitless. But if we can discover and follow the laws which govern prayer, which laws God Himself gave us when He gave us prayer, our prayer life will be sound and normal. And it will bear such fruit as will be a constant incentive to more prayer.

Prayer is such a great effort to most of us because we do not pray right. And for that reason, too, the results are not commensurate with the effort put forth. This is without question the reason for the slothfulness which afflicts so many of those who pray.

People say to themselves: "What good does it do to pray? Nothing happens in my life as a result of prayer, neither in my inner nor my outward life. I know from the Scriptures that without prayer it is impossible to be a Christian; consequently, I must continue to pray. But it is impossible for me to see that anything is accomplished by praying."

At such a time the honest man or woman of prayer is ripe for that instruction in the holy art of prayer which the Spirit of prayer is so willing to give us. Permit me to mention some of the most common mistakes we make when praying, as the Spirit teaches us through the Word.

✠

1. We think that we must help God to fulfill our prayer.

But this has never been God's intention. We are to pray. God Himself will take care of the hearing and the fulfillment. He needs no help from us for that. I know that all very well, I can hear some of my readers saying.

Do not be too sure!

It is remarkable to what an extent we are influenced by the thought that we, by means of our prayers, must help God to some extent to answer our prayers. If nothing more, we at least think that we ought to suggest to God how He should go about giving us the answer. Even though we do not give expression to it, we think about it like this: "Dear God, this is what I am earnestly asking of Thee. I know that it is difficult, but if Thou wilt do so and so, Thou canst accomplish it."

By stating the matter as pointedly as this, I have no doubt caused some of you to object and say, "No one who prays thinks like that when speaking with God!"

But all who have learned to search themselves will admit without any reservation that this is not an exaggeration. It is just this way of thinking which makes prayer so much of an effort and results in so much permanent prayer-fatigue.

Let me take an example from our daily prayer life.

We are praying for two people, let us say, praying that they might be awakened and converted. It is easy to pray for one of them; for the other one it is not so easy.

Why is this so?

Well, the one is by nature, training and temperament such that we think that it is comparatively easy for that person to be converted. In other words, when we see some way for God to fulfill our prayers, then it is easy for us to pray.

The other one, on the other hand, is by nature, training and temperament such that we cannot understand how he or she can be humbled and brought low before God, be persuaded to confess everything, break wholeheartedly with sin and accept the reproach of Christ together with the despised little flock of believers on earth.

Because we cannot understand how God can answer this prayer of ours, it seems hard for us to pray for such a person.

The Spirit of prayer would teach us that we should disregard the question as to whether the fulfillment of our prayer is hard or easy for God. What we think or do not think about this has no bearing on the hearing and answering of prayer. Not only that, it has a blighting and destructive effect upon our prayer life, because we waste our strength on something which is not our concern, and which our Lord has never asked us to be concerned about.

This secret of prayer became very plain to me once many years ago as I was reading the delightful little account of the wedding in Cana of Galilee (John 2:1-11).

Jesus, His mother and His disciples were bidden to the wedding. In all likelihood the family was closely related to, or very friendly toward, the family of Jesus. At least, we notice that the host and hostess had acquainted the mother of Jesus with the embarrassing situation which had arisen when the wine had given out.

Whereupon the mother of Jesus reveals herself as a tried and true woman of prayer.

In the first place, she goes to the right place with the need she has become acquainted with. She goes to Jesus and tells Him everything.

In the next place, notice what she says to Jesus. Just these few, simple words, "They have no wine." Note here what prayer is. To pray is to tell Jesus what we lack. Intercession is to tell Jesus what we see that others lack.

In the third place, let us notice that she did nothing more. When she had told Jesus about the need of her friends, she knew that she did not have to do any more about it. She knew that she did not have to help Him either by suggesting what He should do or anything else. She knew Him and knew that this need had been left in the proper hands. She knew Him. She knew that He Himself knew what He wanted to do.

She knew also that she did not have to influence Him or persuade Him to give these friends a helping hand. No one is so willing to help as He is!

In the fourth place, let us notice that when the mother of Jesus had presented her petition, she had done her part. As far as she was concerned she was through with the matter; she had left it with Him. She was no longer responsible, so to speak, for the embarrassing situation. The responsibility had been placed upon Jesus. It was now up to Him to find a way to help the beloved host and hostess.

She had never before seen Jesus turn water into wine. Therefore she likely did not even think of this way out of the difficulty. It is a question if she, on the whole, even thought about this aspect of the situation. She knew Him well and that He was never at a loss as to what to do. As a rule the way out of difficulty which He chose came as a surprise to her. At least, that was something which did not concern her and in connection with which she did not have to waste any time or effort.

✠

Here is one who truly prays right!

I think we can all see how different our prayer life would be if we would only learn this aspect of the holy art of prayer, with which the mother of Jesus was so familiar.

To most of us prayer is burdensome because we have not learned that prayer consists in telling Jesus what we or others lack. We do not think that that is enough. Instinctively we feel that to pray cannot be so easy as all that. For that reason we rise from prayer many times with heavy hearts. "Can God hear this prayer of mine? Will God heed my humble supplications? And how will He do it? Everything seems so impossible."

Then we go on living in a state of suspense and looking intently for the answer to our prayers.

And when the answer is not forthcoming at once, we think that we must do something in addition to that which we have already done before God can hear us. Just what this something is, we are not certain of in our own minds. And this uncertainty causes that inner anxiety and worry which makes prayer so painful. Especially is this the case if we or some of our dear ones are in great distress and it is imperative that our prayers be heard.

All this is changed when we, like the mother of Jesus, learn to know Him so well that we feel safe when we have left our difficulties with Him. To know Jesus in this way is a prerequisite of all true prayer. This, therefore, is what the Spirit of prayer tries to teach us. It is His work to explain Christ to us and glorify Him (John 16:14).

As we learn to know Jesus in this way better and better, our prayers become quiet, confidential and blessed conversations with Him, our Best Friend, about the things that are on our minds, whether it be our own needs or the needs of others. We experience wonderful peace and security by leaving our difficulties, both great and small, with Him, who is not only solicitous for our welfare but who also understands what is best for us.

And especially will our prayer life become restful when it really dawns upon us that we have done all we are supposed to do when we have spoken to Him about it. From that moment we have left it with Him. It is His responsibility then, if we dare use such a childlike expression. And that we dare to do!

When the Spirit of God has succeeded in teaching us this secret, our prayer life will be freed from a great deal of that inner anxiety and worry which we formerly had when we prayed. After we have prayed, too, we will experience a new peace. We have left the matter in the hands of Jesus, and, like the mother of Jesus, we can go back to our duties secure and happy.* He has taken the matter in hand and is fulfilling our desires.

Instead of our former anxiety and worry we will now often be able to experience a certain childlike inquisitiveness, having left the matter in the hands of Jesus. We will

---

*We shall come back to the question of unceasing and persevering prayer later on in the chapter on "Wrestling in Prayer."

say to ourselves, "It will be interesting now to see how He solves this difficulty."

✠

2. We make use of prayer for the purpose of commanding God to do our bidding.

This is the second great and very common mistake which we make in prayer. But God has never intended that prayer should be used for that purpose. God does not permit us to issue orders to Him. God has not given us His promises and the privilege of prayer in order that we might use them to pound a demanding fist upon the table before God and compel Him to do what we ask.

Let us turn back to the wedding in Cana and follow the course of events further. Again the mother of Jesus gives us some unforgettable advice concerning the right way to pray.

She turned to her Son, as mentioned, and said, "They have no wine." The answer she received was both hard and evasive, at least it seems so to us. Jesus answered, "Woman, what have I to do with thee? mine hour is not yet come."

Imagine for a moment that we had received such an answer. What do you think would have happened? I think we would have said as we so often have done, "Oh, well, I pray; but He does not pay attention to me when I pray." And we would have gone back to our work discouraged.

But look at the mother of Jesus.

She was given a hard answer, a very hard answer indeed. That it was hard was due to the fact, I believe, that Jesus was experiencing a strong temptation at the time. And that from His own mother.

She came and spoke to Him of the embarrassment which was about to confront their beloved host and hostess. Quick action was therefore necessary in order that none of the guests might discover that the wine was giving out. This tempted Jesus to act before His hour had come.

Jesus lived in such a relationship of obedience to and dependence upon His Father that He could "do nothing of Himself" (John 5:19). He, too, when He was to do the will of the Father had to wait for the Father's hour. See John 7:3-6, where He says to His brothers, "My time is not yet come; but your time is always ready."

Jesus felt at the time the temptation to intervene before the Father's hour. It was especially tempting to do this because it was His own mother asking Him to do so. He recognized the tempter, however, at once, even though he came in the garb of His mother; and He cut him off with the harsh word, "Woman." Jesus lets His mother know that when it is a question of the Father's time and will, her position as His mother cannot be allowed to enter into consideration. This harsh word to Mary is exactly in line with the harsh words He spoke to Peter when the latter with well-meant zeal advised Jesus not to occupy Himself with thoughts concerning His own death (Matthew 16:23).

Jesus' mother, then, received a harsh and pointed answer. But at that very time she revealed what a well-trained woman of prayer she was.

In the first place, she submitted humbly to the harsh reply. Not a word did she utter which reflected dissatisfaction or remonstrance. We hear nothing as to whether she understood the reason for Jesus' harsh answer. But whether she understood it or not, she accepted it quietly. She knew that what He said was right and proper, whether she understood it or not.

In the second place, we notice that the harsh answer she received did not shake her conviction that Jesus would hear her prayer and act in the matter. She was so certain of this that she went directly to the servants and said, "Whatsoever He saith unto you, do it." Just what was to take place, she did not know. But that something would take place, she did know. For Jesus had taken the matter into His own hands.

In the third place, and this is the most important for us in this connection, she made no attempt to command Jesus to change the hour of which He had been speaking. She knew Him so well by this time that she would not try anything along that line.

Whether Jesus' mother had tried to do so before, during the long time He lived at home with her in Nazareth, we do not know. It would not surprise us if she had, many times perhaps. In so doing she would have resembled us. But she had gradually learned that it was no use to beg or try to talk Him into intervening immediately. He had His own time and His own hour; and nobody, not even His mother, could change that.

Notice that Jesus' mother had learned this secret of successful prayer: that there is something with which we should not interfere in our prayers, but leave entirely to God, namely, the when and the how concerning the fulfillment of our prayer. This we must leave to Him to determine. Prayer, in other words, should not be used to bring influence to bear upon God, not to speak of nagging God, with respect to the time or the method of hearing our prayer. If we pray in that way, we pray in direct violation of the very idea of prayer, in violation of the laws which govern prayer life.

✠

Most of us have a great deal to learn in this connection.

We are too impatient at all times and not least when we pray. This is especially true when there is something urgent, either with us or with some one who is dear to us. We go to God, speak imploringly to Him and expect Him to intervene at once. The distress of our dear ones and our love for them give us boldness in prayer, and we become almost importunate. Often, too, we have wonderful confidence that God will intervene.

Often, however, impatience will creep into bold and importunate prayers. We plan the whole answer to our prayer. It seems so easy to us. In this particular situation we think that there can be only one thing for God to do if He is to answer our prayer. The answer must come now; it must come immediately. And it must come exactly the way we have planned it.

We arise from our holy meeting with God in prayer, we expect a real answer, and we look for it hour by hour. But nothing happens. The illness and distress that have prompted us to pray take their natural course. No almighty hand seems to stay their ravages!

What disappointments! What discouragement! What weariness descends upon our prayer life after such experiences!

Again we have made use of prayer for something for which prayer should not be used. We have prayed in violation of the laws which govern prayer life. And the consequences cannot be avoided. Prayer has again become a great effort on our part. And we begin to grow tired of praying.

Now notice what we have missed!

Did not God hear our prayer? Indeed He did, and proceeded at once to fulfill it. But He Himself reserved the right to decide when and how the answer was to be given. And in His own time the answer came.

We, however, did not experience it as an answer. We had long since forgotten that we had prayed for this particular thing. At least we did not recognize it as an answer to the prayer we had prayed. We had planned for a very definite answer of our own; and when we did not receive the answer we had planned for, we thought we would receive no answer at all.

We no doubt get many answers from God in this way, answers which we do not recognize as such and from which we therefore do not derive the full joy and benefit, and, above all, answers for which we are not grateful. Our prayer life, in other words, makes us poorer than we really are, because we do not see the answers to our own prayers.

Without question we all feel that we still have a great deal to learn from the Spirit of prayer. And we feel, too, that if He could teach us this little, but important, secret of prayer, our prayer life would be transformed.

We realize also that this deficiency in our prayer life is really due to the fact that we do not trust our blessed Lord.

We think that we understand better than He does when and how our prayers should be answered. Without intending to do so, our prayers become a struggle with God. We make use of prayer to convince God that we see the matter in the right light, that the answer should be given immediately, and should be as we have planned it. Unconsciously we make use of prayer to try to convince God that in this respect we are in the right.

It is this struggle with God which makes us so restless and anxious when we pray. We are afraid that God will not permit Himself to be convinced by our prayers, but will do as He wills regardless of our supplications. I know of nothing that makes our prayer life so burdensome and trying as this does.

When, therefore, the Spirit has taught us that God is unyielding on this point and that He Himself decides when and how our prayers are to be answered, then we will experience rest and peace when we pray. And if the Spirit can teach us also that there is no danger in leaving with Him the time and the means of answering our prayer, our seasons of prayer will become in truth seasons of rest.

We will begin to see that it is God's will not only to hear our prayer, but to give us the best and the richest answer which He, the almighty and omniscient God, can devise. He will send us the answer when it will benefit us and His cause the most. And He will send it to us in that way which will give us the best and most abiding results.

✠

Let me take an example from our daily prayer life.

We pray for our dear ones, especially for the unconverted. We pray day by day, week after week, year after year. But none are converted. If there is any change, it is rather for the worse. They become more worldly, more firmly attached to sin and more callous toward the call of God.

The question arises, "Why does not God hear our prayers?" He hears the prayers of many others. There is, for instance, a family of believing parents who have won all their children for Christ. This makes it even harder and more inexplicable to reconcile oneself to the fact that one's own children are unconverted.

Turning to God and knowing this, your prayers become more fervent than ever; they become almost violent. You tell God that He must save your dear ones, and you tell Him to do so immediately. But you do not feel right when you have prayed like that. No peace and confidence enters your soul, either before or after you have prayed.

Once more you have prayed in direct violation of the laws which govern prayer life. That is why it is so hard for you to pray. You have made use of prayer in order to prescribe to God just when and how He is to save your dear ones.

How our intercessory prayers for our dear ones become transformed when we learn to leave it all in God's hands! Our prayers become quiet, confidential conversations with Him about those we love so much and concerning whom we are solicitous as long as they are away from God.

You will then see wonderful things in your secret prayer room. You will see your eternal High Priest on His knees in prayer. You will see Him beckon to you and ask you to kneel beside Him, and you will hear Him say, "You love these dear ones of yours, but I love them even more. I have created them. I have died for their sins. I have received them in holy Baptism. I have followed them all the way, not only while they as children lived in fellowship with me, but also when they departed from me and entered upon a life of sin. You and I both love them; now let us both pray them into the kingdom of heaven. Only do not become weary and discouraged if it takes time."

Is it not true that such hours spent in secret in conversation with Jesus about your dear ones become truly blessed ones? You rise from such seasons of prayer calm and hopeful, no matter how worldly and obstinate those for whom you are praying may be.

✠

3. We forget to pray in the name of Jesus.

Every believer who has lived with God for some time has had a greater or lesser number of blessed experiences in his or her prayer life, hours when God, so to speak, lifted us up into His lap and drew us unto His own heart, hours when He whispered into our wondering souls words which cannot be uttered. What He told us was really not new either. They were old, familiar things, truths from the Scriptures about the cross and the blood and God's boundless love toward sinners. But it was God who was speaking.

Our hearts were filled with unspeakable joy. We had never realized before that it was possible to experience anything so blessed here on earth.

Then we began to pray. We simply could not refrain from it. Our hearts were full, and it felt so good to speak with

God out of a full heart. It was easy to pray now. We saw God plainly, because we were close to Him. We saw how good He is. That is why it was so delightful to be able to tell Him everything about our sins, our sorrows, our afflictions, our innermost distress, fear and anxiety.

And when we had talked about this, we began to speak with Him about our dear ones. That was just as easy. We had never before felt so safe in bringing our dear ones to God and leaving them with Him.

We did not stop with that either. Everything we thought of became a theme for prayer or thanksgiving. We spoke with God about our relatives and our friends, about believers and unbelievers, and about all the various branches of Christian work. Our hearts were so full of love and solicitude that we would gladly have carried the whole world to God upon the arms of prayer.

We said to ourselves, "I am going to pray differently hereafter. To think that I have up to this time understood so little of the blessed meaning of prayer! Now it shall be otherwise."

And our prayer life did become different. It continued to be different, too, not only for a few days, but for weeks, perhaps months.

Then something happened.

While praying one day we failed to experience our usual joy and the usual zeal which we had been experiencing for some time. We thought, "It will return. Right now I will pray only for the most necessary things. I will intercede for others when the right zeal returns to my heart." Our hearts were so slothful and indifferent that it did not seem possible to begin to pray for all these things again.

But the blessed feeling you had once experienced in your heart did not return. And gradually you fell back into your old ways of praying.

✠

Why did this happen?

Simply because we had not learned to pray in the name of Jesus. Not even when we sat in the lap of God and our hearts were full of the bliss of heaven, did we learn to pray in the name of Jesus. We prayed in the name of our own heart, in the name of our own love and solicitude.

This became very apparent later. When our solicitude had disappeared, our boldness to continue in prayer as we formerly had done also disappeared.

To pray in the name of Jesus is, in all likelihood, the deepest mystery in prayer. It is therefore exceedingly difficult for the Spirit of prayer to explain this to us. Furthermore, it is easier for us to forget this than anything else which the Spirit teaches us.

Scripture speaks of "the mystery of Christ" (Ephesians 3:4).

The name of Jesus is the greatest mystery in heaven and on earth. In heaven, this mystery is known; on earth, it is unknown to most people. No one can fathom it fully.

Behold, we sinners stand in the heavenly light which the Spirit of God has shed upon us. The longer we stand there, the more we see of our own sins, our past life, our unclean thoughts, our impenitent heart, our aversion to God and our desire toward sin.

We know that we must turn to God and that no one else can help us. But the closer we come to God, the worse things seem. We feel that God cannot have anything to do with any one who is as impure and dishonest in every way as we are.

To us the Spirit of prayer says, "Come in the name of Jesus. That name gives unholy people access to a holy God."

We protest and enumerate all the reasons why God cannot receive us. But, sooner or later, light dawns upon our souls. We begin to see what the name of Jesus means and enter into the presence of God with all our sin and with all the impurity and impenitence of our heart.

Then the Spirit says, "Now pray for whatsoever you will. In the name of Jesus you have permission, not only to stand in the presence of God, but also to pray for everything you need."

We raise a number of objections again, "I can not pray. I do not have enough faith. Nor do I have enough love and earnestness. My heart is not spiritual, and I am not sufficiently zealous."

The Spirit listens calmly to all our objections and says, "Everything you say is true. And there would be no hope for you if you were to pray in your own name. But listen again. You are to pray in the name of Jesus. It is for Jesus' sake that you are to receive what you ask for."

✠

Nothing means so much to our daily prayer life as to pray in the name of Jesus. If we fail to do this, our prayer life will either die from discouragement and despair or become simply a duty which we feel we must perform.

What a relief to all those sincere souls who see the unspirituality and worldliness of their own hearts and their lack of faith, love and solicitude, when it becomes clear to them that it is not necessary for us when we pray to work ourselves up to a state of spirituality which we feel that we lack. Nor do we need to put forth any effort to make what little faith we have seem as great as possible. And we do not need to fan the cold embers in our hearts in order to make our waning zeal flare up again.

It is not necessary for us to go through such spiritual gymnastics when we pray.

We need do but one thing: tell God about our condition, about our faith, our solicitude, and our worldly and prayer-weary heart; and then pray in the name of Jesus.

We can come before God and say to Him, "I do not have a right to pray because I do not have a truly prayerful heart. Much less do I have any right to receive what I ask for. Everything which Thou seest in my heart, O Lord, is of such a nature that it must close Thy heart to me and all my supplications. But hear me, not for my sake, nor for the sake of my prayer, and not even because of my distress, for it is a result of my own sinfulness. But hear me for Jesus' sake."

Such souls as these have from time immemorial rejoiced to sing:

> Thy name, O Jesus, beckons me,
> That trusting I shall come to Thee,
> In faith and love on Thee lay hold
> And deep within my heart enfold.
>
> I call upon Thy name each day,
> Where'er on earth I wander may,
> It is for me a house of peace,
> Where from all grief I find release.*

We have learned that to pray in the name of Jesus is the real element of prayer in our prayers. It is the helpless soul's helpless look unto a gracious Friend. The wonderful results which attend prayer of this kind can be accounted for only by the fact that we have opened the door unto Jesus and given Him access to our helplessness.

We have seen above that Jesus wills of His own accord to come in to us and, in His own power, to deal with our needs. It is not necessary for us to constrain Him by our prayers to take an interest in us.

This is another wrong way of praying. When Jesus hears our prayers and intervenes in our distress, He does so because

---

*Translation by P. A. Sveeggen.

His love toward us is free and unmerited, and because He by His suffering and death has purchased and won for us all that we need. And He is now ready at all times to give us these things. He waits only for one thing, and for this He must wait, and that is for us to ask Him to help us. For Jesus will not and cannot force Himself into our distress. We ourselves must open unto Him. And that is the only purpose that our prayers should serve.

The idea is deeply imbedded in all of us that we can by means of our prayers influence God and make Him interested in us, good to us, and kindly disposed toward us, so as to give us what we ask of Him. This is the heathen within us, lifting its head. Among the heathen, prayer is looked upon as a means whereby someone can win the favor of the gods and move them to give away some of their divine surplus.

This same thought flashes upon us frequently when we pray, without our thinking a great deal about it. We feel that there is something God must see in us before He can answer our prayer. We think that He must find an earnest, urgent, burning desire within us in the event that we are praying for something for ourselves. And if we are interceding on behalf of others, we think that He must find a hearty and spiritual solicitude for them in our prayers if He is to hear us. For this reason our prayers often become a soul-exertion by means of which we endeavor to produce within ourselves attitudes which will make an impression upon God.

You have undoubtedly noticed that most of us even change our tone of voice when we pray to God. We adopt a peculiar, pleading, tearful tone of voice. With some it is pure affectation. But this is certainly not the case with most people. It is with them a naive, unaffected, genuine expression of Old Adam's views of God and prayer: When God hears how great our need is, and how urgent it is for us to receive that for which we are praying, He will likely be moved to such an extent that He will yield and let us have it!

A complete revolution with reference to this will take place in our prayer life as soon as the Spirit has taught us to pray in the name of Jesus. He will teach us plainly that what we lack in fervency, solicitude, love and faith are not the things which prevent us from being heard and answered when we pray. These things merely reveal our helplessness. And helplessness is, as we have seen above, fundamental in prayer.

When the Spirit shows us the hardness, the slothfulness, and the indifference of our hearts toward prayer, we now become anxious and confused no longer. Instead, they become added incentives to prayer, that is, the opening of our heart's door to give Jesus access to all our distress and all our impotence.

A new and wonderful thing now occurs. Our seasons of prayer become real hours of rest to our weary souls. They become quiet hours, hours in which we lie at the feet of Jesus and point to all those things which we lack and which make our hearts tired and weary. When our prayer chamber thus becomes a resting place, then we begin to long for it and to look forward to it with joy and anticipation from one prayer session to the next.

This again will result in another change. We will begin to accomplish something in prayer. Joyfully and thankfully we will take up the work of prayer. Our secret prayer chamber will become not only a resting place, but a workshop also.

We shall now proceed to speak about this.

BOOK THREE

Prayer As Work

"Pray ye therefore the Lord of the harvest that He send forth laborers into His harvest."

—MATTHEW 9:38

WHEN Jesus took leave of the eleven apostles at the ascension, He entrusted to them a superhuman task. He charged them to go and make Christ-worshippers of all the nations.

They were to begin in Jerusalem, He had said. That was not far away. The city lay at the foot of Mt. Olivet, and they could see it from where they were standing. In the city were the executioners of Jesus, with His innocent blood upon their hands, ready to annihilate every one who dared to mention the name of the Nazarene publicly. And even though the Eleven should be fortunate enough to escape these murderers, what did they have to preach? A crucified Messiah, a stumbling block to the Jews and foolishness to the Greeks.

As they looked westward from Mt. Olivet beyond the Mediterranean Sea toward Rome, the center of the world, the outlook appeared no brighter. There they would be confronted by the strongest empire which had ever been welded together, the mightiest culture and the richest intellectual life which the world has known to this day.

It was almost irony to send out from Galilee eleven common laborers to win this mighty cultural empire for Christ. True, their number was later augmented by an academically trained co-laborer, Paul; but, he, too, said that he was determined not to know anything or preach anything, even in the great cultural centers, save Jesus Christ and Him crucified.

But He who sent them knew what He was doing. He had equipped them for their superhuman task in a twofold manner.

Objectively, He had equipped them with the Messianic gift itself, the Holy Spirit, through whom the powers of the whole supra-mundane world were put at the disposal of the little Christian congregation. We shall not, however, discuss this phase of the subject at this point.

Subjectively, He had equipped them with prayer, the means by which all of these objective, supra-mundane powers are imparted to the individual believer and to the congregation.

We get a vivid impression of how highly He Himself evaluated this equipment when we read a few of His statements about it.

"If two of you shall agree on earth as touching anything that they shall ask, it shall be done for them of my Father who is in heaven" (Matthew 18:19).

"For verily I say unto you, If you have faith as a grain of mustard seed, ye shall say unto this mountain, Remove hence to yonder place; and it shall remove; and nothing shall be impossible unto you" (Matthew 17:20).

One of those who had had the opportunity to make use of this equipment throughout a whole lifetime of work and sacrifice says of it, "In nothing be anxious; but in everything by prayer and supplication with thanksgiving let your requests be made known unto God" (Philippians 4:6).

He who had sent them knew that this weapon, this piece of equipment, would make them invincible. "Nothing shall be impossible unto you," were His words. When at His ascension He took leave of His friends as far as His physical presence was concerned, He extended His almighty arm so far down that we insignificant and sinful people can reach it every time we bend our knees in prayer.

Whenever we touch His almighty arm, some of His omnipotence streams in upon us, into our souls and into our bodies. And not only that, but, through us, it streams out to others.

This power is so rich and so mobile that all we have to do when we pray is to point to the persons or things to which we desire to have this power applied, and He, the Lord of this power, will direct the necessary power to the desired place at once.

This power is entirely independent of time and space. In the very moment that we bend our knees and pray for our brethren and sisters in Zulu, Madagascar, Santalistan, China, or the Sudan, in that same instant this power is transmitted to these people. Here is an example of wireless transmission of power which transcends the dreams of the boldest inventor.

This weapon is the more valuable to the friends of Jesus, because it is not possible for the enemies of Jesus to make use of it. True, His enemies can lay hands on the weapon; but the moment they grasp it in earnest they are transformed from enemies to friends of Jesus.

Here, too, we see divine grace and wisdom.

How terrible this weapon would become if it could be used by anybody and everybody for purposes of revenge and destruction! Instead He has decreed that only His own friends can establish contact with these inexhaustible sources of power. In fact, the means of contact has been devised so carefully that the connection is automatically cut off, even to the friends of Jesus, as soon as they try to employ this power in ways contrary to the will and purpose of Jesus. It is only when we pray for something according to the will of God that we have the promise of being heard and answered.

✠

It is our Lord's will that we who have received access to these powers through prayer should go through this world transmitting heavenly power to every corner of a world which needs it sorely. Our lives should be, according to our Lord's plans, quiet but steadily flowing streams of blessing, which through our prayers and intercessions should reach our whole environment.

And it is taken for granted that we, too, like His friends, will "begin in Jerusalem" and then go farther and farther "unto the uttermost part of the earth."

It is His will that we should begin at home. As we go in and out among our dear ones day by day, we should transmit to them by intercessory wireless that supernatural power which will enable them to lead victorious lives and which will put thanksgiving and joy into their hearts and upon their lips, instead of a series of disheartening defeats, bringing discouragement to both body and soul.

We should say to God as we mingle with our dear ones each day, "God, give them each Thy blessing. They need it, because they live with me, and I am very selfish and unwilling to sacrifice very much for them, although I do love them."

Then there would be a good spirit in our homes. For God hears prayer. Heaven itself would come down to our homes. And even though we who constitute the home all have our imperfections and our failings, our home would, through God's answer to prayer, become a little paradise.

There are many believers who make failures of their homes. Their children seek all their pleasure and enjoyment outside the home and do not thrive at home. If our Lord could speak to the people in such homes and tell them what He would like to say, the very first thing would most likely be this, "Ye have not, because ye ask not."

It is our Lord's will also that we should include our neighbors in our prayers. As soon as we see them in the morning we should say to God, "Lord, bless my neighbors today. Give them according to their several needs!"

How unhappy the relationship between neighbors often is! As a rule trouble begins with little things, either a sheep, or the chickens, or the dog, or a fence, or a piece of road. First misunderstanding, then offence, then unfriendliness, then enmity and finally a lawsuit.

If we will employ the holy magic of intercession, our relations will gradually become amicable even with neighbors who are otherwise obdurate and difficult to deal with.

In some countries the people still greet each other when they meet at work with the deep and beautiful salutation, "God bless your work!" It is possible that this greeting has become trite from steady usage, as all forms of greeting, with the result that people no longer think of what they are saying. But when this greeting first came into use, people felt a real desire to ask God to bless the labors of their co-workers.

We, too, should have the same desire. We know that it is not always easy to work. At times it can be exceedingly hard. For this reason we should take the opportunity when we meet people at work to pray down upon them some of that supernatural power which will make their work easier and productive of greater results.

Wherever we go, we meet people who are in need of something. If the Spirit could give us that open eye of love which sees both visible and invisible needs, everything we saw would give rise to prayer. We would turn to the Lord and tell Him the needs both of our friends and of our enemies. That is how He would like to have us pray. It is written, "Pray without ceasing" (1 Thessalonians 5:17).

Gustav Jensen, the cathedral provost, on one occasion related the following incident.

A little church was being built a few years ago in Oslo. In that connection the cathedral pastor tells of a believing business man who lived on the outskirts but had his office in the heart of the city. This business man would leave home a few minutes earlier than usual each day in order to spend a little time at the scene of construction. There he could be seen day after day in quiet prayer for the laborers, for the edifice, for those who were to minister in the church and for those who were to hear the Word of God there.

That man had learned to pray as a means of working with the Lord.

My aunt told about a captain who visited their home one day. As they sat conversing happily about their experiences in the Christian life, the captain suddenly arose, went over to her, and, placing his hands upon her head, uttered a fervent prayer for God's blessing upon her.

Here was another man who had learned how to pray.

Now, I do not mean that we should imitate the captain and begin to go around laying our hands on each other's heads. But I do wish that we had some of that loving zeal which he had, and that we shared his views on the uses to which prayer may be put.

Do you not think that it is the Lord's will that we should make use of our right to pray for people every time we meet them, even though we have never met them before and have not even made their acquaintance? I think that our Lord expects us to make use of every opportunity to impart such gifts, even though it be the only time we meet, supramundane gifts mediated by our prayers.

Some will possibly raise the objection that this is not practicable, that I am overdoing and exaggerating. But I cannot see that this is the case. I firmly believe that we are unsuccessful in prayer because we are too slothful and because we are not diligent enough in prayer. If the Spirit of God could fill us with holy zeal, we would soon find time and opportunity to breathe a sigh of prayer to God for such people.

We think quickly. Passing rapidly by a person on the street we find time and opportunity to make critical remarks to ourselves about that person. It takes place almost automatically, because our evil nature is asserting itself. Just think if the Spirit of God could make the new nature within us so strong that we would automatically lift our hearts in prayer to God every time we met someone!

One of my missionary friends had just returned from the mission field. We were sitting conversing about many things, among them also about his health during the years he had been out on the field. This is a difficult problem in the lives of most missionaries. The tropical fevers weaken and undermine the health of many of them, even in the early years of their life. And my friend had been at a station where the fever had been particularly bad.

When I began to talk about this, he was a little evasive. But I was so well acquainted with him that I was not afraid of being inquisitive; and I asked him how his health really had been. He replied as follows:

"When I was about to sail for the mission field, I naturally went around to my friends in my home community to say good-bye. In this connection I called on an elderly believing woman in a tenant household. As I bid her good-bye, she clung to my hand and, looking me calmly in the eye, said quietly, 'I am going to pray to God for you and ask Him to save you from the fever in order that you may devote all your strength to your work out there.'

"And I have not felt the fever once during all these years," he added, with tears in his eyes—tears of joy!

Here was another woman who had learned to make use of prayer as a means of doing the Lord's work. There are many ways in which we can work for missions, even for us who do not go to the mission fields. God grant that we might see this and act accordingly; it would make it easier for the missionaries to work out there.

✠

Prayer is the most important work in the kingdom of God.

It is our Lord's will that we should enter into this work as soon as we have been won for God. We should by prayer enter into the work which has been begun by our Christian parents, and for which they have sacrificed, suffered, striven and prayed. We should enter into it and build upon their work, first and foremost by means of prayer. Permit me to mention some phases of Christian work in which the work of praying is important, indeed, where prayer is the only instrumentality which can be employed.

The first which must be mentioned is prayer for workers.

Jesus' own words show us this: "The harvest indeed is plenteous, but the laborers are few. Pray ye therefore the Lord of the harvest, that he send forth laborers into his harvest!" (Matthew 9:37-38). Our first task is to get the workers whom the Lord desires for the various tasks in His vineyard. Let us particularly notice that this should be done by means of prayer.

No doubt many believers have not paid much attention to this part of our prayer-work. We pray for those who have entered into Christian work. We pray also perhaps for those who are preparing to enter some kind of Christian work. But most of us have not reached the point where we pray for those who, as yet, are neither in the work, nor preparing for it, but for whom the Lord has some definite work in mind. The words of Jesus which we have cited tell us that God does not call and send forth these workers into the harvest without our prayer.

The greatest danger in Christian work is no doubt that workers go out who have not been sent by God. The work they do is merely human work, even though it be carried out with great personal power and ability and highly systematized efficiency.

There are people on the foreign mission fields who should never have been there. Some of them have not even been converted to God. And at the same time there are people here at home who should have been missionaries.

This is our own fault. We should have prayed about this important matter, prayed that none might be sent out who were not sent of God; and at the same time that those whom God has chosen might not remain at home but really go out into foreign lands.

The same is often true of our pastors.

We complain often that we have so many unqualified pastors. It is comparatively easy to complain. What we really should complain most about is ourselves and our own slothfulness in prayer. We should, according to Jesus, have a part in deciding who are to become pastors. But instead of that we sit idly by and accept the pastors who come to us. We leave it to young men only eighteen years of age to decide who are to become the pastors in our church.

This must not be allowed to continue.

According to the words of Jesus, believers not only have the right, but it is also their duty to have a part in pointing out who are to become pastors and who are not. This is work, however, which can be done only on our knees.

Believing friends, let us take up this work!

Reflect for a moment, and you will see what it would mean to our church and our people. Hundreds, thousands of pastors, faithful pastors, believing pastors, pastors filled to overflowing with zeal for souls! Pastors sent by God, scattered throughout our whole country!

Some smile disdainfully, others sigh disconsolately at such a thought. Perhaps it would be best for all of us to ponder anew the words of Jesus: "Pray ye therefore the Lord of the harvest, that he send forth laborers into his harvest." "Nothing shall be impossible unto you."

This is also true of our teachers.

We have many good teachers in our country. But, unfortunately, we also have many who are neglectful of their work, and whose work is actually harmful to the souls of our children. Here, too, we have been negligent. We have not continued humbly and regularly to pray God that believing Christian young people might attend those schools which prepare for teaching and take up this important and responsible work. When we get a poor teacher and we complain about it, I think our Lord would like to say to us: "Ye have not, because ye ask not."

In general, we should, by means of prayer, help to bring out the gifts of grace which God has given to Christian people.

✠

A neighborhood or a community may, for instance, lack a good leader. Instead of complaining about the poor leaders we do have, we should pray forth the gift of leadership which is needed.

In another community they may have a capable leader, but lack local gifts of grace for the preaching of the Word. We should again consider the words of Jesus: "Pray ye therefore the Lord of the harvest, that he send forth laborers into his harvest."

Finally, we should on bended knee pray for the evangelists who go about preaching the Word of God. However, we neglect this work of prayer, too. The result is that we have evangelists who never should travel and preach. They are not sent by God, but by people.

At the same time we have farmers, fishers, craftspeople and business persons who have been chosen of God to be preachers, but whom He cannot send forth into the great harvest, because we do not pray forth these gifts of grace.

In this connection permit me to mention what an ordinary country girl, Bolette Hinderli, was able to accomplish for the great preacher of God, Lars Olsen Skrefsrud.

In a vision she saw a prisoner in a prison cell. She saw plainly his face and his whole form. And a voice said to her, "This man will share the same fate as other criminals if no one takes up the work of praying for him. Pray for him, and I will send him out to proclaim my praises among the heathen."

She was obedient unto the heavenly vision; she suffered and prayed and fought for this prisoner, although she did not know him. She waited longingly, too, to hear of a convict who had become converted and called to missionary work.

Finally, during a visit in Stavanger, Norway, she heard that an ex-convict who had been converted was to preach in the city that evening. When Skrefsrud stepped up to the speaker's stand, she recognized him immediately as the one she had seen in her vision.

This woman had learned the meaning of Jesus' words about praying forth the gifts of grace.

As far as I am able to understand the Word of God, and as far as I can learn from the history of the kingdom of God, no prayer-task is more important than this. If the right people get into the right places, there is almost no end to what they can do. Think of men like Martin Luther, Hans Nielsen Hauge, Lars Olsen Skrefsrud, Hans Peter Börresen, William Carey, Hudson Taylor.

John the Baptist is introduced in the Bible in the following words, "There came a man, sent from God" (John 1:6). Then something always happens, regardless of whether the person concerned is highly gifted or not.

Some might ask why God does not bring forth and send out these gifts of grace without our prayer. What little I am able to say in answer to this question I shall reserve for a later chapter where we shall discuss some of the problems connected with prayer.

✠

A part of our labor in prayer must also be devoted to our leaders.

They have a great responsibility. A leader must have not only wisdom and experience, but also great personal courage, enabling him or her to dare to act according to his or her own convictions and not merely according to the desires of a majority. It often requires a great deal of strength and perseverance to carry out the things one believes to be the will of God, and to do so even when the opposition is triumphant and friends grow weary.

It is easy to criticize leaders. After the thing is done, everybody is wise. Then we all see how it should have been done. Beforehand nobody sees what ought to be done, but that is just when leaders must act. Let us pray for our leaders at all times instead of constantly criticizing them.

By this I do not mean that we should accept uncritically everything decided by the leaders. If you think they are making a mistake, tell it to them in humility and in love. Above all, pray for them. Pray for them until they themselves are convinced that they have made a mistake. Thereby you will have succeeded in having your viewpoint adopted and, in addition, the spirit of comradeship and love of the community will have won a great victory.

We should also pray for those who preach, for the pastors and the evangelists.

It is hard to be a preacher. In the first place, there is a great responsibility involved in preaching the Gospel, in rightly dividing the Word. In the next place, preachers are exposed to unusually many and great temptations. They are tempted along two lines in particular: either to conceit or to discouragement, all depending upon how well they succeed or how badly they fail in their work as preachers.

If you hear preachers who appear to you to have become conceited, pray God earnestly that they may become so humble and poor in spirit again that they can feed the flock of God. On the other hand, if you hear preachers who are getting discouraged, ask God to give them new courage.

Pray especially for Christian people with gifts of grace in your community. Pray them forth. Pray that they may be given courage to continue with unflagging zeal from year to year. There are signs which indicate that the local gifts of grace in our churches are beginning to languish and that in some places they have practically died out. Pray ye, beseech God that such a misfortune may be averted.

In general, pray a great deal especially for the local preachers, that they may not feel that they are superfluous. Pray for the power of God upon them. You will find that they will bring you a fresh message from heaven, even though they are not highly gifted and do not have a particularly striking way of presenting their message.

We should pray also for our meetings.

Here, too, our sins of omission are great. In planning for meetings we unquestionably pay the least attention of all to the preparations which should be made by prayer.

How are our meetings usually prepared? Well, first we decide where the meeting is to be held. Then when it is to be held. Next we secure a speaker. Finally we arrange to have the meeting well advertised. Everything is in readiness, we assume, and all we have to do is to wait for the meeting to begin.

Immediately before going to the meeting we pray for the services, if we have time. As a rule, however, Satan sees to it that we do not get time. Many come late to the meeting. Others come in good season. Do the latter make use of the time to pray for the meeting? No; as a rule they whisper about this, that and the other thing until the time is up and the meeting begins. Someone offers prayer, and the preaching begins.

And still we wonder why we see so little fruit as a result of our meetings and our work! Hell laughs and heaven weeps over such meetings. Again the sad words of Jesus recur to us, "Ye have not, because ye ask not."

Oh, if the people of God could see the work which should be done in prayer before the meetings! They themselves would be blessed much more richly than they now are, and the meetings would become centers of divine power in which wonderful things would take place.

The most remarkable thing would be that the sermons would not be a bit more wonderful than they were before, but there would be a new power in them. The Word would strike home to the consciences of believers and unbelievers alike with greater effectiveness.

Finally, we have intercessory prayer for the unconverted.

This part of our labors in prayer is perhaps the one we understand best and carry out best. Most believers long for a spiritual awakening. The desire to see souls saved is the impelling motive in nearly all the Christian work of our day. In this respect awakenings are always the order of the day now. People speak a great deal about revivals. Much is done to bring them about also. And not a little praying is done with this in mind.

We notice, too, that God now and then sends us an awakening.

Nevertheless there is something in this connection which we should think about, especially with reference to our prayers. In the first place, I would point out the fact that awakenings occur very seldom. As a rule decades elapse between revivals in our cities and rural communities. In the next place, I would make mention of the fact that the revivals which do take place are usually not very great, being limited to a single locality. Finally, I would say that they are often representative of but very little spiritual power. By this I do not mean that there are no powers at work. There are often tremendous, almost brutal powers at work. But it becomes apparent, often during a revival, and especially afterwards, that there was much human power and but little divine power in the work that was done.

The reason for all this is that we fail to labor in prayer.

We long for revivals; we speak of revivals; we work for revivals; and we even pray a little for them. But we do not enter upon that labor in prayer which is the essential preparation for every revival.

Many of us misunderstand the work of the Spirit in the unconverted. We think that this work is limited essentially to the time when the awakenings are taking place. We seem to think that the unconverted are not subject to divine influence between times.

This is a complete misunderstanding. The Spirit works without interruption, during awakenings and between awakenings, even though He works differently, and the effect therefore also is different in people's hearts.

The work of the Spirit can be compared to mining. The Spirit's work is to blast to pieces the sinner's hardness of heart and frivolous opposition to God. The period of the awakening can be likened to the time when the blasts are fired. The time between the awakenings corresponds, on the other hand, to the time when the deep holes are being bored with great effort into the hard rock.

To bore these holes is hard and difficult and a task which tries one's patience. To light the fuse and fire the shot is not only easy but also very interesting work. One sees "results" from such work. It creates interest, too; shots resound, and pieces fly in every direction!

It takes trained workers to do the boring. Anybody can light a fuse.

This fact sheds a great deal of light upon the history of revivals, a history which is often strange and incomprehensible.

There are many people who would like to light the fuse. Many would like to be evangelistic preachers. And some preachers are even so zealous that they light a fuse before the hole has been bored and explosive matter put in place. The resulting revival becomes, therefore, nothing but a little display of fireworks!

During a revival our zeal for souls is so great that we are all active. Some are so active that they are almost dangerous during an after-meeting. When, on the other hand, the awakening has subsided, and everyday conditions, perhaps even dry seasons, return, then most of us lose our zeal and cease our activity.

But that is just when the Spirit calls us to do the quiet, difficult, trying work of boring holy explosive material into the souls of the unconverted by daily and unceasing prayer. This is the real preparatory work for the next awakening. The reason why such a long period of time elapses between awakenings is simply that the Spirit cannot find believers who are willing to do the heavy part of the mining work.

Everybody desires awakenings; but we prefer to let others do the boring into the hard rock.

There are, God be praised, in every community some who take up this work which tries one's patience so sorely. The Lord reward you, brother and sister, and, above all, give you grace to persevere in the holy work which you have taken up!

✠

In this connection I would like to say a few words also about how we should pray for awakenings.

If the Spirit of prayer can give us real zeal for souls, we will want to have a part in praying for an awakening in the widest sense of the term, a world-awakening. We see that that is just what the world needs now more than anything else. Many of us are asking almost despairingly, "Where will it all end: the bitter class hatred and class conflict; the steadily mounting competition between the nations for money and power, brought on by their greed for plunder; the secret building up of competitive armaments among the world powers; the public and private disregard of the Law of God and the gospel of our Lord? Where will it all end if we do not have a revival so far-reaching and general that it will stem the tide of sin in all parts of the world and open up new avenues for the gospel in the frivolous and wicked generation which today peoples our earth?"

Prayer for a spiritual awakening in the midst of our present needs will formulate itself as a prayer for a nationwide awakening. Our national life is a living organism, an unbroken continuity from one end of the country to the other. Mammonism, the dance craze, pleasure-madness, immorality, drunkenness, lawlessness and disrespect for the Word of God are sins which are leavening our entire population, in the city and in the country, from top to bottom.

There is no way in which this unholy tendency can be arrested and our nation saved from atheism, rationalism and skepticism except by means of a quiet, sound and yet powerful spiritual awakening, reaching all levels of society in every city and rural community.

However, an all-inclusive prayer for a general awakening must always be accompanied by prayer for an awakening in our own neighborhood, our own city. Here, too, we must remember to "begin in Jerusalem." It is within our own circle that we as individuals have our greatest responsibility. And only by being faithful in this can the Spirit set us over greater and farther-reaching prayer objectives.

Our prayer for a spiritual awakening will without question be most effective if we take up the work of interceding for certain individuals in particular.

We find that most of us who have been converted have had someone praying for us, someone who carried us personally to the throne of God while we were unconverted. It seems to me that no one is so poor as an individual for whom not a single soul is praying, and who has no one who takes him or her personally and persistently to God in prayer.

We should enter into this work and become personal and regular interceders for certain definite individuals. Ask the Spirit of prayer to assign to you the individuals for whom you should pray. If every believer would do this, the Spirit would distribute the unconverted in every community among the believing men and women of prayer; and ultimately there would not be a single soul but what some consecrated and faithful believer would be praying for him or her.

Then it would not be easy for the unconverted to continue to live in sin! Holy spiritual explosive materials would be planted into their souls daily, and the ground blasted from beneath their unrepentant lives.

Revivals come to those cities and communities which have believers who have taken up the holy work of intercession. A spiritual awakening cannot be brought about by force, and not by magic either. The Lord will send it as soon as it is spiritually possible to do so. In some places the battle is long and hard, and the opposition cannot be overcome except "by prayer and fasting," as Jesus says in Mark 9:29.

In some places prayers are fulfilled in the form of a mighty storm of spiritual awakening; in other places like a gentle breeze. In the latter instance the number awakened at one time is never very great, only one or two. But, on the other hand, quiet awakenings of this kind continue for a long time, often several years. I hear, now and then, on my travels of a few places where the revival never comes to an end, so to speak. The Lord adds to them day by day those that are saved, as is so beautifully written of the first Christians in Acts 2:47.

We should thank God for awakenings no matter in what form He sends them. But it appears to me that they give promise of being especially fruitful when they come like a gentle breeze.

✠

Before bringing to a close this section on prayer as work I would like to underline the fact that it is a labor for which there is no substitute in the kingdom of God.

We all need to be reminded of this because it is easy for us to look upon it in exactly the opposite way. We are inclined to think that when we are real busy in the work of the kingdom of God, then we can without danger spend less time in prayer. This way of thinking is in our very blood. And Satan sees to it that it is quickened into life at just the right time.

It is, therefore, necessary for the Spirit of God to burn into our hearts this mystery, that the most important work we have to do is that which must be done on our knees, alone with God, away from the bustle of the world and the plaudits of other people.

This work is the most important of all, because it is prerequisite to all the rest of the work we have to do in the kingdom of God: preaching, pastoral work, meetings, societies, administrative groups, organization and solicitation of funds. If the labor of prayer does not precede, as well as accompany, all of our work in the kingdom, it will become nothing but human work, more or less capably done and with more or less effort and agitation as the case may be, but resulting in nothing but weariness both to ourselves and to others.

The work of praying is prerequisite to all other work in the kingdom of God, for the simple reason that it is by prayer that we couple the powers of heaven to our helplessness, the powers which can turn water into wine and remove mountains in our own life and in the lives of others, the powers which can awaken those who sleep in sin and raise up the dead, the powers which can capture strongholds and make the impossible possible.

✠

There are no doubt many believers who have not given much attention to prayer as work. Prayer is looked upon mainly as a means of sustaining our life in God from day to day in the midst of an atmosphere which is so worldly that it almost chokes to death our weak, frail, spiritual life. And we pray accordingly. We move in a narrow circle about ourselves and those nearest to us. Now and then we widen the circle a little bit, especially when we gather with the people of God, and the mighty tasks of the kingdom of God at home and abroad are placed before us. But when we get back home into our daily routine, our prayer-circle narrows down again.

Only the Spirit of prayer can teach us to labor in prayer, to employ prayer as a means of doing spiritual work. Every time we see how selfish and slothful we are in prayer, we should cry in our helplessness to Him who giveth gladly and upbraideth not. He can create, that is, bring into being that which is not. God be praised!

One of the things that the Spirit must teach us about prayer as work is this: to learn to take time to pray.

All work takes time. When it becomes clear to us that prayer is a part of our daily program of work, it will also become clear to us that we must arrange our daily program in such a way that there is time also for this work, just as we set aside time for other necessary things, such as eating and dressing.

Intercessory prayer of the kind indicated above will necessarily require time. No one else, therefore, will be able to do it except those who are willing to sacrifice the time to do it. This alone is sufficient to make it clear to us that the work of intercession can be done only by those who are willing in spirit. All others will find more than enough excuses for not doing it. One excuse will be that they have not the time and cannot arrange to take the time.

If the work of prayer is to be successful, it must also be properly planned.

Lack of proper planning will be enough to make the prayer life of many unproductive and ineffective. They have no definite times for prayer, only seasons of prayer as time and occasion permit. Everything is left to the whim of circumstance. And the things they pray for are determined in the same haphazard way, depending in the main upon two things, first, the amount of time they have for prayer and, second, what they at the moment happen to remember to pray for.

We all know, of course, what the result is. The enemy of our souls sees to it that we "get" so little time to pray that what we are able to accomplish in prayer is reduced to a minimum for this reason alone. Furthermore, he also sees to it that we become distracted so as to forget the things for which we should especially pray.

That will never do; the labor of prayer requires a definite plan and purpose.

I must know what work I have to do in my secret prayer chamber before I enter into it, what persons and what branches of the work of the kingdom of God I am to take to God in prayer. As the Spirit deepens our solicitude and widens our prayer-circle, we will find many things for which to pray. Such a thing as my occasional forgetfulness must not be allowed to hinder me from doing this work. If it is difficult for me to remember every individual person and each particular cause for which I should pray, I must come to the assistance of my memory by making a note of them.

Johannes Johnson, a great Norwegian missionary, once told of a missionary's wife who little by little permitted herself to be trained in the holy work of prayer. As a result she found more and more things for which to pray. At last she was unable to remember them all. So she went to work and resolutely wrote them all down in a notebook.

When she was about to pray, she simply took out her little notebook and spoke with God about the one thing after the other which she had noted down. Thus she continued to pray for a large number of people and many Christian enterprises. As soon as she was given something new for which to pray she wrote it down in her little book. And as the Lord granted her prayers, she crossed out the entries in her book and wrote in the margin, "Thanks."

I have never had much faith in the old prayerbooks with their prayer formulas for morning, evening and special occasions in life, although they, too, have no doubt been helpful to some people. But I would recommend most highly prayerbooks of this kind.

This way of praying may easily become schematic and a mere matter of routine. It is therefore important to make prayer as personal as possible. If we summarize and generalize when we pray, our prayers will have a tendency to become impersonal. In praying for some person one should mention something definite in his life or in his relationships. In praying for a Christian organization one should make mention of the workers connected with the enterprise as well as the special difficulties or tasks confronting them from time to time.

This makes it easier for us to pray. Our prayers become more personal. They become more concrete than the general prayer for God's blessing or help. This is the thought that Luther brings out also by stressing the idea that we should pray for something definite.

If we take up the work of prayer in this way, it will become self-evident that time will be required, so much time that it will be scarcely possible for us to include all our prayer objectives in our prayers every day. We will, therefore, naturally divide them among the six days of the week. And then include them all when Sunday comes, because on that day we have a great deal more time for prayer. Of course, all of us will at various times have certain persons or things especially upon our hearts, which will lead us to pray for them every day.

✠

The Christians of our day are busy people.

We do not live for nothing in the century of work. Never in the history of God's church have His people worked more than now. And never before have we had so many workers. Never has the work been so well organized as it is today.

The work, too, is being divided more and more. Every branch is being organized. Day by day the work goes on, a work which is very exacting and which requires stupendous effort. Sacrifice after sacrifice of time, energy, interest and money must be made in order to accomplish the task.

A serious difficulty arises from the fact that there are many branches of Christian work, all of which make their appeal to practically the same people. And the number of people to whom the appeals are made is really not very great either.

When times get hard, it becomes difficult for most of these people to spare both the time and the money to support these many activities. As a result competition arises, which is being felt more and more. And as a further result many of the workers become not only weary but even embittered.

The machinery of Christian work has become large and complicated.

Many are already clamoring loudly for retrenchment. Nothing new must be started. And the work that we have must be curtailed if it is at all possible.

Others are not quite so radical. They ask for more organization. We live in the age of organization. They think that better organization will bring the needed relief.

Others again have no suggestion to offer as to how a catastrophe may be averted. All they do is to sigh and wonder how long it all can last.

As I look at the situation today in our voluntary Christian organizations, such thoughts as these do not come to my mind.

We are all no doubt agreed that there is a disparity between the machinery and the motive power. But to me it does not seem natural to remove this disparity by reducing the amount of machinery, as long as it is possible to increase the amount of power and thus equalize things in that way.

I can remember the time when the threshing machine was run by hand in my home community. Several shifts were necessary, and the work was very strenuous because the machine had to be driven as fast as possible.

Now on the other hand it is being done differently. By means of modern motive power a hundred times as much is threshed each day. And the workers need not work as much now as they did before. It is the power that makes the difference. It threshes, sifts and cleans the grain all in one operation, and saves the work of many people.

I often think of this when I observe the situation in the Christian enterprises of today. That the machinery has become too heavy is due to the fact that we are operating it with human labor instead of running it by power from above. I know full well that there is not a little individual, as well as united, prayer. But I am afraid that we do not put real work into prayer, and that we do not, therefore, put our trust in the power of God when it is a question of carrying on and carrying forward our work. And for that reason our Christian work becomes so strenuous and so exhausting.

The powers of heaven are at our disposal.

Have we made the proper contacts with these powers? Let us pray for the Spirit of prayer. He will take us into the workshop where the power conduits lie. Above the door of this room is written: "Nothing shall be impossible unto you."

The future of the Christian work which is now being carried on with such great intensity does not depend upon curtailment or re-organization.

It depends upon whether the Spirit of God can persuade us to take up the work of prayer.

BOOK FOUR

Wrestling in Prayer, I

"Watch and pray, that ye enter not into temptation."

—MARK 14:38.

MOST of us cannot quite understand how prayer can involve difficulty and anguish. Why should praying entail so much suffering? Why should our prayer life be a constantly flowing source of anguish?

If we will reflect but for a moment, we will, however, see that it really cannot be otherwise. If prayer is, as we have seen, the central function of the new life of faith, the very heart-beat of our life in God, it is obvious that our prayer life must become the target against which Satan directs his best and most numerous darts.

He understands better than we do what prayer means to ourselves and to others. That is why his chief attack is directed against our prayer life. If he can in one way or in another weaken it, his prospects of stealing our life in God without us even noticing it are of the very best.

This is not only the most painless way of stealing from us our spiritual life; it is also the quietest way, the way which creates the least sensation. Satan desires above all to provide himself with servants who think that they are God's children and who are even looked upon as children of God by others.

For this reason Satan mobilizes everything that he can commandeer in order to hinder our prayer. He has an excellent confederate in our own bosoms: our old Adam. Our carnal nature is, according to the Scriptures and our own bitter experience, enmity against God (Romans 8:7); and our old nature realizes that it can expect nothing but mortification every time we really approach God in prayer.

It is important for us to bear this clearly in mind. By so doing we will, in the first place, be able to account for something which we formerly could not understand, namely, the aversion to prayer which we feel more or less strongly from time to time. Our disinclination to pray should not make us anxious or bewildered. It should merely substantiate to us the old truth that the "flesh lusteth against the spirit." We shall have our carnal natures with us as long as we live here below, and we must endure the discomfiture occasioned thereby.

We should deal with the unwillingness of our flesh in this respect in the same way as we deal with all the other sinful desires of our flesh. We should take it to God and lay it all before Him. And the blood of Jesus Christ will cleanse us from this sin as it does from all other sin.

In the second place, we must keep the hindrance to prayer, which we have at all times within our own bosoms, constantly in mind, or else our prayer life will most certainly ebb out. The thing to remember is that our carnal nature, which is enmity toward God, will not refuse directly to participate with us in prayer. If this were the case, our warfare against our flesh would be comparatively simple.

On the contrary, the protest of the carnal mind against prayer is made indirectly, very cleverly and at the opportune time. Instinctively and automatically it will mobilize all the reasons it can conceive of for not praying now: You are too busy; your mind is too preoccupied; your heart is not inclined toward prayer; later on you will have more time, your mind will be more calm and collected, and you will be able to pray in a more devotional frame of mind.

Finally you decide to pray, but all of a sudden the thought comes: I must do this thing first. When I have finished this, I shall be ready for a good season of prayer.

Then you do the thing you have in mind. And when you have done it, your mind has become distracted. One thing after another begins to clamor for your attention. And before you know it, the whole day is gone, and you have not had a single quiet hour with God.

Thus our carnal nature aligns itself against prayer, day in and day out. And the man or woman of prayer who is not mindful of this cannot avoid becoming a victim of the stealthy tempter. As long as we think we will "get" time to pray, we still do not know a great deal about our own carnal natures.

That our wrestling is not against flesh and blood but against the spiritual hosts of wickedness in the heavenly places (Ephesians 6:12), we see plainly when we begin to take notice of the outward hindrances which are placed in the way of our prayers from day to day.

When those hours of the day come in which we should be having our prayer-sessions with God, it often appears as though everything has entered into a conspiracy to prevent it, human beings, animals and, above all, the telephone. It is not difficult to see that there is a veiled hand in the complot.

Woe to the Christian who is unacquainted with these foes!

The first and the decisive battle in connection with prayer is the conflict which arises when we are to make arrangements to be alone with God every day. If the battle is lost for any length of time at this point, the enemy has already won the first skirmish.

But even though we do gain the victory at the threshold of our prayer chambers, our prayer-struggle is by no means over. Our enemies will pursue us deliberately into our very prayer rooms. And here our carnal natures and Satan will take up the battle anew, though from a somewhat different angle.

Our carnal natures will be just as afraid of meeting God now as before we went into our prayer room. Now every effort will be concentrated upon making our prayer session as brief as possible, or upon distracting us so completely that we are not even now given an opportunity to be alone with God.

My friend, do you know anything about this battle?

As you kneel to speak with your Lord, it seems as though everything you have to do appears vividly before your mind's eye. You see especially how much there is to do, and how urgent it is that it be done, at least some of it. As these thoughts occur, you become more and more restless. You try to keep your thoughts collected and to speak with God, but you succeed only for a moment now and then.

Your thoughts flit back and forth between God and the many pressing duties which await you. Your prayer hour becomes really the most restless hour of the day. Your mind is literally torn to shreds. Joy, peace and rest are as far from you as the east is from the west. And the longer you prolong the session, the more you feel that you are neglecting your work. To put it plainly, you feel as though the time you are spending on your knees is just that much time wasted. Then you stop praying.

The enemy has won a very neat victory!

Here is where we are face to face with enemies who are vastly superior to us. And they will defeat us every time, without any doubt whatsoever, if we do not learn the true secret of prayer: to open our hearts to Jesus and give Him access to our needs. Prayer is for the helpless, as we have seen above. And helplessness is not a hindrance, but an incentive, to prayer. Nor will our helplessness in connection with our restless thoughts and our distracted minds be a hindrance to prayer when the Spirit has succeeded in teaching us the little, but important secret of prayer, that my helplessness is Jesus knocking at my heart's door, the little sign He is giving me, the little message that He is sending into my poor soul to tell me that He desires to enter in and employ His powers to relieve my distress.

He has power also over my restless thoughts. He can rebuke the storm in my soul and still its raging waters.

There is a profound and beautiful passage bearing on this in Philippians 4:7, "And the peace of God, which passeth all understanding, shall guard your hearts and your thoughts in Christ Jesus."

The only way in which we can gather and keep collected our distracted minds and our roaming thoughts is to center them about Jesus Christ. By that I mean that we should let Christ lay hold of, attract, captivate and gather about Himself all our interests. Then our sessions of prayer will become real meetings with God. Just as the radii of a circle run to the center, so all our thoughts should run toward God.

The apostle says that the peace of God will have this effect upon our restless thoughts. I shall find no rest and peace in prayer as long as I think that I, by the concentration of my own will, can keep my thoughts on God. But as soon as I realize that I am helpless, also when it comes to the question of controlling my restless thoughts, and let Jesus, my Almighty Friend, deal with these powerful foes of my soul also, then the peace of God will descend with healing and blessing upon my distracted soul. Then the Spirit will be able to explain and glorify Christ anew to my soul. And—well, then my thoughts will be laid hold of and taken captive by Christ, attracted to Him, and centered upon Him.

✠

Why should we have definite seasons of prayer?

Is not this a hangover of salvation by good works? Isn't it because people desire to merit something before God by praying many times? Isn't it because people think that they can acquire greater merits the more often they present themselves before the All-Highest, pay Him their respects and bring Him their plaudits?

Of course, it can be done in that way. And many, no doubt, do look upon prayer as a service which they render to the Lord, because they think that to do so is in accordance with His desires in the matter.

But let us nail this one thing down: We do not need definite seasons of prayer for God's sake. He does not need them. On the contrary, it is we who need them.

I know that there are people who say that set times for prayer tend toward formalism and unspirituality, and that it is better to look to God in prayer whenever, during the course of the day, we feel inwardly impelled to pray, whether we are working or are at leisure. Then prayer will be a freer and more voluntary means of communication between God and our souls, they say.

To this I would reply that the two types of prayer need not be mutually exclusive. On the contrary, they should supplement each other.

Later on, in the chapter on the form of prayer, I shall discuss the topic of unceasing prayer in detail, and I shall not, therefore, deal with it any further here. I would, however, at this point like to say a few words about the necessity of having definite times for prayer each day.

There is something about our soul-life which makes this necessary. It is very true that we should, in the midst of our daily work, wherever we are, and at any time, look to God and tell Him what is on our hearts. But there is one thing we do not attain if we limit ourselves to this, and that is quietude.

Even Jesus, who all the time lived in unbroken prayer-fellowship with His Father, found it necessary to withdraw from the multitude and from the bustle of life in order to be alone and gain quietude. See Mark 1:35; Matthew 14:23;

Luke 6:9, 12, 18, 29; 22:41. Contact with the world and with the multitude distracts us and scatters our thoughts.

For that reason it is necessary for us to withdraw at regular intervals and enable our souls to attain that quietude and inward composure which are essential if we would hear the voice of God.

We are not all spirit, and we are therefore dependent upon outward things and conditions. Only to be alone means a great deal to us. When no one hears or sees us, then we are really ourselves in the presence of God. Then no one can influence us in any way, and we need not pay deference to anyone.

Quietude, even in the purely outward sense, means a great deal to our inward composure. Not until we have come apart from those things which divert our attention to outward things, are our souls free to engage in inward activity. Or perhaps we should speak first of that inward, passive state known as the devotional attitude. As soon as outward things lose their distracting influence over our soul-life, God Himself can attune our souls to prayer, because we are in a devotional attitude.

This attitude can be compared to a forerunner, who announces the coming of God to us. In this, too, we see God's gracious dealings. It is His divine presence which attunes our distracted, worldly and earthly-minded souls to prayer.

Many who pray are not aware of this. As soon as they enter into their secret chamber they begin at once to speak with God. Do not do that, my friend. Take plenty of time before you begin to speak. Let quietude wield its influence upon you. Let the fact that you are alone assert itself. Give your soul time to get released from the many outward things. Give God time to play the prelude to prayer for the benefit of your distracted soul. Let the devotional attitude, the attitude of holy passivity, open all the doors of the soul leading into the realm of eternal things.

✠

We are on the whole disposed to emphasize activity in prayer too much. From the time we begin and until we have finished, we are busily engaged in speaking with God. And we feel almost as though there is something wrong or something lacking in our prayer if we do not talk continuously to God.

There is activity in prayer, of course, and it includes speaking with God. But that should not be all. In the quiet and holy hour of prayer we should also be still and permit ourselves to be examined by the Physician of our souls. We should submit to scrutiny under the holy and penetrating light of God and be thoroughly examined, spiritually fluoroscoped and X-rayed, in order to ascertain just where our trouble lies.

We all know that light, both natural and artificial, has marvelous healing properties. In recent times especially they have begun to utilize these properties in the therapeutic treatment of various diseases. We now have light-ray treatments in which the affected part is exposed to strong, regular rays of various kinds.

The ailment which afflicts human souls cannot be cured except by light-ray treatment. The light of heaven must enter into our souls, and every affected part must be exposed to its rays. It is not sufficient to submit to a light-ray treatment of this kind only during the period of awakening and conversion, during which time every secret nook and corner of our souls is exposed to the light of God, and all our sins, both old and new, are brought to light to be confessed, forgiven and put to death. This arrests the disease, but it does not eradicate it. The light-ray treatment must continue daily, as long as we live here on earth.

Our quiet hours with God should be daily light-ray treatments of this kind. But they do not get to be that for all of us. We talk to God about many things, many good things; and we talk all the time. But when we are through talking, for a longer or a shorter period of time as the case may be, we say Amen and go our way.

Supposing you did this at the doctor's office. Suppose that when your turn comes, you enter into his office. He offers you a chair. Then suppose that you sit down and begin to tell him about all your pains and troubles. And then when you have talked a long time, suppose you get up, bid a polite adieu and leave. What would the doctor think? Well, that is hard to say, but most likely he would think that some demented person had been in his office by mistake.

God has multitudes of such patients in His waiting room every day. That is one reason, too, why our seasons of prayer mean so little to us. We go out just as we came in. No doubt God regrets to see us leave the Great Physician of our souls without even seeking or receiving any advice concerning our ailment.

When we go to our meeting with God, we should go like a patient to the doctor, first to be thoroughly examined and afterwards to be treated for our ailment.

If you have a pain deep down in the most sensitive region of your soul, your conscience, then point it out to Him. If you do not know just where the pain is, but know that you have a pain somewhere within you, and that you have no peace, then take all the time you need. Let Him examine you with His Roentgen ray.

Say as the psalmist did of old:

> "Search me, O God, and know my heart:
> Try me, and know my thoughts;
> And see if there be any wicked way in me,
> And lead me in the way everlasting."
>
> (PSALM 139:23-24.)

Then something will happen when you pray.

You will begin to see things in your life and in your heart which are inimical to your spiritual life and detrimental to you as a worker in the Lord's vineyard. You will experience a time of reckoning which will bring you both tears and rejoicing. But it will send you back to your work, not only with new peace and assurance, but also with new power. "For the eyes of Jehovah run to and fro throughout the whole earth, to show himself strong in the behalf of them whose heart is perfect toward him" (2 Chronicles 16:9).

✠

This, however, does not occur without a struggle.

It is the work of the Spirit to convict of sin. The quiet hour of prayer is one of the most favorable opportunities He has in which to speak to us seriously. In quietude and solitude before the face of God our souls can hear better than at any other time.

Behold, He speaks to us about our sins, the sins which we love the most, and with which it is easiest for us to make an alliance. No child of God can enter into an open covenant with sin. We do, however, make secret alliances. We try to make ourselves believe that the little thing that is bothering us is not sin. We excuse and defend our actions.

To illustrate.

I can imagine that the Spirit spoke to you in your quiet hour about money. Little by little you had drifted into a wrong attitude toward money. And the Spirit spoke to you about it, earnestly and persistently.

When you read the Word of God, for instance, it happened, remarkably enough, that you ran across passages again and again which dealt with that very thing, money. When you heard the Word, the same thing happened. It seemed as though all the preachers in the world had entered into a sworn compact to speak about Mammon.

But matters became worse than ever when you turned to God in prayer. It seemed as though the Spirit would not talk about anything else. You prayed as usual, but the Spirit said quietly and authoritatively, "Money! Money! Money! The prayers you are offering up are vain. God desires to speak with you about your financial affairs. And if you do not care to talk about them, you may as well save yourself the effort of your words and your petitions."

Do you remember the terrific struggle which took place in your soul?

There was something within you which said that the Spirit was right. But you would not yield. You excused and defended your financial dealings. You said to yourself that you were not stingy; you were merely practicing economy.

When your wrestling with the Spirit of God became too intense, do you remember the Satanic device to which you resorted in order to get rid of these pointed accusations? You changed over to intercessory prayer. You began to pray for others. Verily, the human heart is more deceitful than anything else!

The secret prayer chamber is a bloody battleground. Here violent and decisive battles are fought out. Here the fate of souls for time and eternity is determined, in quietude and solitude, without another soul as spectator or listener.

To pray is to open one's heart to Jesus.

But if I close my heart at one single point where the Spirit is making sin a living reality to my conscience, then I have shut Jesus out from my whole heart. I have ceased to pray, even though I continue to try to deliver myself of something which I think is prayer in order to ease my troubled conscience and gain relief from the restlessness of my soul.

Here is where many a praying soul has lost the decisive battle. The Spirit of prayer has had to forsake them, putting them out of the ranks of those who really pray.

This book may fall into the hands of some one who has suffered this evil fate. In that event, I would like very much to call attention again to the words with which we began: Jesus stands at the door and knocks. He desires to enter in anew. You can be raised up from your fallen estate. You feel that you have sinned grievously, because you have been very bold in your deceitfulness. And I realize that that is true. But listen again to the words as they are recorded: "If any man hear my voice and open the door, I will come in to him."

Will you open the door?

You no doubt understand what Jesus means by that figure of speech. Will you acknowledge as sin that which you formerly excused and defended? That will be letting Jesus come in to the horrible distress and impotence caused by that secret sin of yours. And He will drive the strong one out of your unhappy soul.

✠

If, finally, we were to sum up the conclusions to which we have come so far in our discussion of wrestling in prayer, we could, no doubt, do so by saying that there is only one issue at stake in the whole struggle, even though the battle be fought along somewhat different fronts. It is this: All wrestling in prayer must bring us into harmony with the Spirit of prayer. For, as we have already seen above, all our difficulties in prayer arise from the simple fact that we are not in harmony with the Spirit of prayer. Our prayer is too often a wrestling with the Spirit of prayer. From this it is easy to understand why our prayer life becomes burdensome and strenuous, also why we achieve no results, why our prayers are not heard, and, finally, if our prayers are one continuous wrestling with the Spirit of prayer, why He must depart from us and, as a consequence, leave our whole prayer life to wither and die.

The real purpose of our wrestling in prayer is, therefore, to render us so impotent and helpless, not only in connection with our physical and spiritual needs, but, above all, our inability to pray, that our prayer really becomes a prayer for the Spirit of prayer. No matter what we pray for, whether it be temporal or spiritual things, little things or great things, gifts for ourselves or for others, our prayers should really resolve themselves into a quiet waiting for the Lord in order to hear what it is that the Spirit desires to have us pray for at that particular time.

Everyone who is experienced in prayer knows that to listen quietly and humbly for what the Spirit of prayer says requires continued and powerful wrestling.

It requires wrestling, in the very first place, in order to hear and obey the Spirit's admonitions to prayer. Indeed, this involves both watching and wrestling, as Jesus says in Mark 14:38; because the spirit is willing to pray, but the flesh is weak. But then, too, the soul who prays, who listens and gives heed to the Spirit's promptings concerning prayer, will experience what a joy prayer is when we pray in harmony with the Spirit of prayer and not in opposition to Him.

There will, in the next place, be a struggle involved in listening to what the Spirit has to say also while we pray. The most difficult thing for us in this connection is, without doubt, to listen to what He has to say about our sinful habits. It also requires daily wrestling and watchfulness to listen to the Spirit when He speaks to us about the various persons and things He would have us remember in prayer.

But when this becomes the one thing needful to us when we pray, we shall also find that it is actually possible for us to pray, even though we are often altogether too worldly and earthly-minded; and that prayer is not something far beyond us, the privilege of only a select few. It begins to dawn upon us that prayer is essentially a question of the Spirit of prayer. But about this we wish to speak at greater length in the last chapter.

BOOK FIVE

Wrestling in Prayer, II

> "Now I beseech you, brethren, by our Lord Jesus Christ and by the love of the Spirit, that ye strive together with me in your prayers to God for me; that I may be delivered from them that are disobedient in Judea."
>
> —ROMANS 15:30-31.

THESE words of the apostle afford us a glimpse into another aspect of the struggle involved in praying. He speaks in this passage of intercessory prayer taking the form of a struggle. He has given expression to the same thought in slightly different words in Colossians 4:12-13, "Epaphras, who is one of you, a servant of Christ Jesus, saluteth you, always striving for you in his prayers, that ye may stand perfect and fully assured in all the will of God. For I bear him witness, that he hath much labor for you, and for them in Laodicea."

This kind of wrestling in prayer has often been misunderstood.

It has been conceived of as a struggle in prayer against God, the thought being that God withholds His gifts as long as possible. They must be wrung from Him in one way or another. And prayer is looked upon as a means by which God can be made to relent, and be moved to give us an answer to our prayers. And if our prayers do succeed in accomplishing this, it is because we have fought with God, stormed Him with supplications, convinced Him by our crying needs, and, on the whole, persevered until He has yielded.

It is not necessary to be very familiar with the Bible in order to know that this view of wrestling in prayer is pagan, and not Christian.

God is Himself good. It is not necessary for us to pray or wrestle in prayer in order to make God kind or generous. "God . . . giveth to all liberally and upbraideth not" (James 1:5). He is not only good; He is also omniscient, knowing at all times what is best for us. It is not necessary for us to try to teach Him what is best for us by argumentation, persuasion, or much talking.

✠

The idea that to wrestle in prayer is to wrestle against God is usually based upon certain passages of the Scriptures. Jacob's wrestling with God as recorded in Genesis 32:22-32 is one of those passages. Here we are told how Jacob struggled with God. He refused to give up, saying, "I will not let thee go, except thou bless me." And God did bless him. However, he strained the hollow of his thigh as a result.

The New Testament passage usually cited is the one about the struggle which the Canaanitish woman had with Jesus (Matthew 15:21-28).

Here we are told of a woman of Gentile ancestry who met Jesus near Tyre. She asked Him to heal her daughter who was grievously vexed with a demon. But Jesus did not answer her a word. The disciples, however, interceded for her saying, "Send her away, for she crieth after us." Then Jesus replied, "I was not sent but unto the lost sheep of the house of Israel."

But the woman was in great distress and would not give up. She came and worshipped Him, saying: "Lord, help me."

Still Jesus did not relent, answering her in such hard words as these, "It is not meet to take the children's bread and cast it to the dogs." Still the woman refused to yield. Quickly but humbly she seized upon Jesus' own metaphor about the dogs, saying: It is not necessary to take the bread away from the children and give it to the dogs; they will be perfectly satisfied with the crumbs which fall from their master's table.

Then Jesus yielded and granted her supplication.

It cannot be denied that both of these accounts on first thought seem to lend support to the idea that the soul which wrestles in prayer must actually overcome God and compel Him to fulfill the petition.

However, we shall soon see that such an interpretation of these passages will bring us into conflict with the teaching of the whole Bible concerning both God and prayer. And for that reason we must try to find an interpretation which is in harmony, both with what God is, and what prayer is, as this is proclaimed to us throughout the whole Bible. Let us consider this briefly for a moment.

Why did not Jesus answer the woman when she asked Him so meekly for help? Because He did not care for her? No, and no again!

And when the disciples interceded for her, why did Jesus make reference to the idea that He had been sent only to the chosen people? He had made exceptions to this rule before, in Matthew 8:5, for instance.

That Jesus did not do this because He wanted to be contrary, is clear to everyone who has learned to know Jesus. When He, nevertheless, followed the strange procedure which He did, it was because He had a special purpose in so doing.

Everyone who has walked with Jesus for some little time and has had some experience in prayer-fellowship with Him, knows that this is not a unique instance, but one which recurs from time to time in the lives of all believers.

Jesus answers not a word.

We cry, one time after another, each time more loudly and more vehemently than the time before. But not a word from Jesus. After some time has elapsed, He speaks. But the words we hear are sharp, stern words from the Scriptures, piercing to the dividing of our very joints and marrow, in the same way as His words about the dogs fell upon the ears of the Canaanitish woman. Or as He said to His own mother at the wedding in Cana: "Woman, what have I to do with thee?" Or as He answered the nobleman of Capernaum: "Except ye see signs and wonders, ye will in no wise believe" (John 4:48).

Why does Jesus utter such hard sayings?

Is it not written that "He giveth liberally and upbraideth not" (James 1:5)? Yes, He does; and without upbraiding. The words He speaks to us may be sharp, but He does not use them in order to offend us. His strange and often incomprehensible way of dealing with us is prompted by His love, which is so great that He not only desires to give us what we ask for, but much more. As Luther says, "We pray for silver, but God often gives us gold instead."

Every time Jesus sees that there is a possibility of giving us more than we know how to ask, He does so. And in order to do so He often has to deal with us in ways which are past our finding out.

He answers not a word to our many supplications. Will He then not hear us? Yes, He will; He began to hear us from the very moment that we began to pray. But if He had given us the things we prayed for immediately, He would not have succeeded in giving us what He had appointed for us.

We find a typical illustration of this in the eleventh chapter of John.

Lazarus had become ill, and the sisters had sent Jesus this beautiful message concerning their brother: "Lord, he whom thou lovest is sick." And the sisters rejoiced to think that Jesus would hurry and come and heal their dear brother.

But Jesus did not come.

Lazarus became worse and worse; he died, and they had to bury him.

It was a trying time for those two sisters. Why did not Jesus come? Had He not had mercy upon all who asked Him for help? Why did He not come to their home now? Did He not care for them any longer? Did He not understand how much it meant to them to have Lazarus recover? And now it was too late! Their brother was not only dead; he was already buried, and his body had begun to decay.

They did not understand what it all meant. Worst of all, they could not understand how Jesus could deal with them as He did.

Now, why did Jesus deal with them in this way?

Jesus had from the very beginning decided to help them. He had also decided forthwith to give them more than they asked of Him. That is why He delayed His coming until Lazarus was dead and buried. He wanted to raise him from the dead.

Why did He want to do this?

In the first place, because by so doing He could manifest more of His power, more of the "glory of God," as He Himself calls it in verse forty. In that way they would receive not only what they asked for, the restoration of their brother to health, but their faith and trust in Jesus would also be strengthened and deepened.

In the second place, He could in this way teach them a lesson in true humility. He could point out how impatient they had been, and how they had murmured against him. How had they not during those endless days and nights upbraided Him both in thought and in word. At least, we notice that both sisters began at once to upbraid Jesus as soon as He arrived: "Lord, if thou hadst been here, my brother had not died" (John 11:21, 32).

It is very possible, because of the intimate associations which Jesus had had with this little family, that they had developed a more or less conscious feeling that they were privileged characters as far as He was concerned. Had not Jesus made it manifest that He prized in a special way their faith and love towards Him?

During the long days of waiting, however, the glamor of it all had completely disappeared. Jesus had not, after all, appreciated their love and their faith very highly. Thus they reasoned, and with it went the last vestige of their pride. And that is why the answer to their prayers and the great resurrection-miracle appeared doubly great to them when they did take place.

Jesus had somewhat the same thing in mind with the Canaanitish woman when He delayed and postponed the answer to her prayer, first by remaining painfully silent and then by using some sharp, harsh words. He wanted to give her more than a healed daughter. He wanted to give her something for herself besides.

He knocked at her heart's door with words that were both tender and harsh with love. And He succeeded in His loving purpose with her. She opened her heart to Him.

At first, neither His silence nor His words offended her. Both convinced her of her true condition. Then she took the attitude which Jesus wanted and expected her to take. She threw herself at His feet and surrendered to His mercy in the simple and yet touching words: "Lord, help me!"

There, at the feet of Jesus, she takes humbly to heart also the hard words about the dogs. Behold, a truly humble soul, "humbling herself beneath the mighty hand of God."

Upon receiving her daughter back again, healed by the words of Jesus, she is saved, not only from her temporal distress, but also from a selfish and demanding spirit. As a humble sinner she has learned to cast herself upon the unmerited grace of God.

Jacob's "wrestling" with God must be understood in the same way.

Let us notice first that it is God who meets Jacob to wrestle with him, in the form of a man. Jacob fears Esau, but God desires to show him that he is in much greater danger than that. God is against him. It was reconciliation with God which was being forced upon Jacob that night.

God desired to bless Jacob. He had already chosen him to be a patriarch of the chosen people. But the blessing had been withheld, because Jacob had sinned both against God, against Esau and against their aged father. It was these sins that God desired to speak with Jacob about at this time. It was no doubt this matter which was being settled in Jacob's heart while the outward struggle was going on.

Jacob thought, presumably, as all the rest of us, that God is reluctant about giving us His gifts and, therefore, must be overcome in wrestling. He used, too, the very significant expression: "I will not let thee go, except thou bless me."

But God was ready to bless Jacob whenever Jacob was willing to confess his sins and be reconciled to God. And the same thing happened to Jacob as happened to the others of whom we have just spoken. He received more than he asked for. He prayed that God would help and bless him and his household in the critical struggle with Esau which was before him, a struggle in which Esau, impelled by hatred and revenge, might vanquish and exterminate Jacob and his whole family.

God gave him more than this. He gave him a meeting with God which Jacob never forgot. The event left such an impression that the whole people of Israel preserved the memory of it. Henceforth they never ate the sinew of the hip which is upon the hollow of the thigh of any animal. This they observed in commemoration of the fact that the sinew of Jacob's hip had been strained that fateful night.

God gave Jacob something which made him humble the rest of his life. It made him insignificant in his own eyes and dependent upon God. And Jacob's weakness in this respect became his best defense against the enemies he had made for himself by his insistent, cunning and ungovernable nature.

After this inquiry, let us return to the striving which the apostle exhorts us to engage in when we pray for others.

After what we have seen, it has become clear to us that we cannot interpret this either to mean that we can compel God to give an answer to our prayers which He is reluctant to give. Much to the contrary, our struggling must be in line with the wrestling we have just described. The only difference is that in the wrestling we have already discussed the prayers concerned ourselves, while, in the striving mentioned by the apostle, our prayers are for others.

Our intercessory prayers involve much striving on our part for exactly the same reasons as we have mentioned in the preceding pages. There is something about God's attitude toward our prayers for others which is hard and often impossible to understand. And that is what precipitates the struggle.

Our striving is a struggle, not with God, but with ourselves.

There are things in us which are a hindrance to our intercessory prayers. These hindrances are what the Spirit of prayer points out to us, and immediately the struggle begins. Permit me to mention the following:

First and foremost, our selfishness.

The real hindrance to intercessory prayer is, of course, the fact that we live and move in such a narrow circle about ourselves and those nearest us that the Spirit of prayer cannot create in our hearts true zeal for others. The result is that our labors in intercessory prayer often become very circumscribed, and in many cases utterly impossible.

However, the Spirit can convict us also of this sin. And as soon as I acknowledge my selfish indifference, He will save me from it. The Spirit of prayer will then fill my empty heart with holy zeal and remind me of one thing after another for which I should make my poor and humble intercessions!

But if we wish to preserve this Spirit, we must be willing to struggle.

Jesus said, "Watch and pray, that ye enter not into temptation: the spirit is indeed willing, but the flesh is weak." Without holy watchfulness we will soon lose our zeal for others. All watchful intercessors know themselves and therefore keep close to Him who daily fills their hearts with loving zeal for others.

Secondly, our love of ease.

Jesus saw clearly this danger to our prayer life. He has spoken of it in Luke 18:1-8. The passage begins in this way: "And he spake a parable unto them to the end that they ought always to pray, and not to faint." Likewise, let me remind you of how ruefully He upbraided the apostles in Gethsemane: "What, could ye not watch with me for one hour?"

It was love of ease which overcame the apostles that night. And it is love of ease which overcomes us. We begin by praying for something for ourselves or for others, and all goes well until our love of ease begins to make itself felt.

Then we get tired of praying, and little by little our praying ceases. How many such humiliating experiences can we not all look back upon!

That is why Jesus admonishes us to watch and pray. The apostle speaks of it as striving in prayer. When he says of Epaphras that he was always striving in prayer for the believers in Colossae, we see what it means to strive in prayer. If we desire to retain our zeal for those for whom we are praying, and if their needs and distress are to move us to intercede for them daily, we will find that this does not take place without striving and wrestling on our part.

The most difficult prayer, and the prayer which, therefore, costs us the most striving, is persevering prayer, the prayer which faints not, but continues steadfastly until the answer comes. To strive in prayer for a person or for a cause means, in the first place, to live, feel and suffer with that person or that cause. That alone requires a great struggle, especially if we are not related to the person concerned by ties of blood or friendship.

In the second place, to strive in prayer means to struggle through those hindrances which would restrain or even prevent us entirely from continuing in persevering prayer. It means to be so watchful at all times that we can notice when we become slothful in prayer and go to the Spirit of prayer to have this remedied. In this struggle, too, the decisive factor is the Spirit of prayer.

Let this be our consolation and our encouragement: The Spirit of prayer will put into our hearts the various things for which we should pray and keep our attention focused upon them, provided we will be candid and alert and will confess to Him that we are fainting in prayer whenever He makes us aware of the fact.

Notice how graciously, after all, God has designed prayer for us!

Let us also notice the inner connection between laboring in prayer and striving in prayer.

The Spirit can persuade none of us to take up the work of prayer as described above unless He can also persuade us to strive in prayer. And this is again, after all, the reason why it is so difficult for God to get enough people to do the work of prayer. But about that we shall speak at greater length later on in the chapter about the School of Prayer.

✠

Prayer and fasting.

In Mark 9:29 Jesus says, "This kind can come out by nothing, save by prayer and fasting."

Here Jesus introduces us to the greatest struggle connected with prayer.

While Jesus and three of the apostles were on the Mount of Transfiguration, a man had brought his son, possessed of a dumb spirit, to the other apostles. The latter had tried to cast out the evil spirit, but they had not succeeded. When Jesus came down, the father brought his son to Him, and Jesus healed the boy. As soon as the apostles had come into the house and were alone with Jesus, they asked Him why they could not cast out the evil spirit. To which Jesus replied, "This kind can come out by nothing, save by prayer and fasting."

Before inquiring into the relationship between prayer and fasting, we must briefly explain what is meant by fasting.

To fast is to abstain from eating and drinking for a shorter or longer period of time.

Fasting was enjoined by law in Israel. The whole nation had to fast on a certain day of the year (Leviticus 16:29). After the captivity several annual days of fasting were introduced (Zechariah 8:19). And the Pharisees went so far that they fasted twice each week (Luke 18:12).

The Hebrew word for fasting signifies the humble submission of the soul to God, the Holy one. For that reason it was observed on the great day of atonement when the people effected their great annual reconciliation with God and otherwise upon occasions of national disaster (Judges 20:26, Joel 2:12, Jonah 3:5) or mourning (1 Samuel 31:13).

Jesus did not abolish fasting; He lifted it from the legalism of the Old Covenant into the freedom of the New. Fasting is an outward act which should be carried out only when there is an inner need of it (Matthew 9:14-15). Furthermore, Jesus warns against fasting as a means of displaying piety, so as to be seen of others (Matthew 6:16-18).

But should *we* fast?

This is no doubt a live question in the minds of many Christians in our day. Many look upon fasting as a part of the outward ceremonialism which belonged only to the Old Covenant. That free, evangelical Christians should fast is entirely strange and foreign to their way of thinking.

So far from the teachings of Jesus and the apostles concerning fasting have we strayed. It is no doubt high time that we feeble, weak-willed and pleasure-loving Christians begin to see what the Scriptures say concerning this element in our sanctification and in our prayer life.

Fasting is not confined to abstinence from eating and drinking. Fasting really means voluntary abstinence for a time from various necessities of life, such as food, drink, sleep, rest, association with people and so forth.

The purpose of such abstinence for a longer or shorter period of time is to loosen to some degree the ties which bind us to the world of material things and our surroundings as a whole, in order that we may concentrate all our spiritual powers upon the unseen and eternal things.

Fasting in the Christian sense does not involve looking upon the necessities of life, which we have mentioned, as unclean or unholy. On the contrary, we have learned from the apostle that nothing is unclean of itself (Romans 14:14). And that food has been created by God to be received with thanksgiving (1 Timothy 4:3). Fasting implies merely that our souls at certain times need to concentrate more strongly on the one thing needful than at other times, and for that reason we renounce for the time being those things which, in themselves, may be both permissible and profitable.

Fasting is, therefore, entirely in line with what we have said above about the necessity of having quiet and secluded seasons of prayer, is in reality only a prolongation of the latter. None of them have been ordained for God's sake, but for our sakes. It is we who need to fast. A great deal could be said about this, but we must limit ourselves to the meaning of fasting in connection with prayer.

We take as our starting point the thought which we have come upon again and again in our inquiry: The one great secret of prayer is the Spirit of prayer. The most significant thing that we can do in connection with prayer is to establish contact with the Spirit of prayer. To strive in prayer means in the final analysis to take up the battle against all the inner and outward hindrances which would dissociate us from the Spirit of prayer.

It is at this point that God has ordained fasting as a means of carrying on the struggle against the subtle and dangerous hindrances which confront us in prayer.

Fasting must be voluntary, Jesus says.

We Christians resort to fasting when we find that some particular thing is acting as a hindrance to our prayers. This may be some special difficulty of which we are cognizant and which we feel as a hindrance, or it may be something that we do not understand. All we know is that there is something impeding our intercourse with God in prayer.

We resort to fasting in order to set our distracted and worldly-minded souls free for a time from material things and the distraction of our environment, and thus give the Spirit an opportunity to search out our whole inner being and speak with him about the things which are grieving the Spirit of prayer, in order thus to re-establish unhindered communication with the Spirit of prayer and a greater influx of divine power.

✠

Let us now consider briefly those circumstances in life in which Christians feel the need of fasting.

In the first place, during special temptations.

When Jesus was to be tempted in a special way, immediately after He in Baptism had been endued with power for His ministry, He fasted. Note the fact that He fasted a long time, forty long days. So seriously did Jesus take His struggle against temptations. This is a reminder to us of how indifferent we are about the temptations which assail us.

Even Jesus, who was sinless, felt the need of acquiring composure of soul by fasting before He entered the lists against Satan.

After the miracle of the loaves in the desert, when the people desired to make Him king, we notice that Jesus immediately resorted to fasting again, though in a shorter and simpler form, by denying Himself His night's sleep (Matthew 14:23) in order to acquire concentration of soul through undisturbed communion with the Father and thus be fully endued with power to meet the tempter who was again pursuing Him.

Our temptations have acquired, and are maintaining, a great deal of power over us because we have not sought the divine nearness and holiness which fasting affords, and which would enable us to deal radically differently with our temptations.

In the second place, Christians feel the need of fasting before making a decisive choice.

When Jesus was to choose His apostles, a choice fraught with great significance to the whole world, He spent the whole preceding night alone with the Father in prayer (Luke 6:12). Although Jesus maintained an unbroken relationship of obedience to His Father, and although His spiritual senses had never been blunted by sin, nevertheless He felt the need of concentrating His soul in the quiet of the night upon uninterrupted communion with His Father in order to be certain that He would be following the Father's leading when He made His choice the following day.

In this connection I might also mention the little incident which is recorded in Acts 13:2, "As they ministered to the Lord, and fasted, the Holy Spirit said, Separate me Barnabas and Saul for the work whereunto I have called them." While the apostles were fasting, the Spirit spoke to them the decisive words which sent Paul out upon his first missionary journey, the words which started the whole missionary movement to the Gentiles.

We would not make so many rash and unspiritual choices, nor would we be so frequently at a loss what to do in the face of important decisions, if we would begin to fast in the Christian sense, and thus give the Spirit of prayer an opportunity to speak to our souls. We are too often occupied with outward things, and as a result we often become very hard of hearing spiritually.

In the third place, fasting is useful in the planning and carrying out of exceedingly difficult tasks.

In Acts 13:3 and 14:23 we read of how the first Christians prepared themselves by fasting for important acts in the congregation, such as ordaining elders and sending out missionaries. The purpose of this was evident enough. They wanted to concentrate spiritually and put themselves wholly and completely at the disposal of the Spirit of prayer in order that, by prayer and the laying on of hands, they might mediate the grace which the Spirit desired to impart to those chosen.

These early, Spirit-filled Christians felt the need of this; we earthly-minded, overly-busy, and spiritually poverty-stricken Christians of today have put aside fasting entirely. We feel that we do not need it!

Of course, fasting is and must be voluntary. Only the Spirit of prayer can make us so humble that we gratefully make use of all the means that the Lord has given us.

In the fourth place, fasting is useful before great and mighty acts.

Jesus said, "This kind can come out by nothing, save by prayer and fasting." Thus He explains why the disciples were powerless in dealing with demoniacal possession on this occasion. We are told here, too, that there are differences in mighty works. Some require more power from above than others.

Jesus shows here that fasting is the means whereby believing prayer can mediate the accession of needed power from God.

To make use of a rather mechanical, but nevertheless vivid illustration, we might compare this with the transmission of electrical power. The greater the volume of power to be transmitted, the stronger the connection with the power house must be, that is, the larger the cable must be.

As we have seen above, prayer is the conduit through which power from heaven is brought to earth. Jesus says in effect that the greater the volume of power to be transmitted from above, the stronger must be the prayer cable which unites the soul with God.

How does this take place?

As we have mentioned again and again, everything depends upon the Spirit of prayer. Our prayers are rendered ineffectual in the same degree as they take a different course than that in which the Spirit would lead us. And they become even more impotent when we come in conflict with the Spirit and grieve Him.

Fasting helps to give us that inner sense of spiritual penetration by means of which we can discern clearly that for which the Spirit of prayer would have us pray in exceptionally difficult circumstances.

At the same time it helps to cleanse our souls of any impure motives which might be present when we pray for mighty acts. This cleansing takes place when we, in the quietude and concentration of fasting, discover the love of honor and other impure motives which lie concealed in our prayers, and when we receive power to confess these things to the Lord, saying, "I would rather that the miracle be not permitted to take place than that I by taking honor unto myself should defile Thy name and desecrate prayer. But if Thou canst perform the miracle without my disturbing or desecrating anything that is Thine, then grant it, Lord."

BOOK SIX

The Misuse of Prayer

"Ye ask, and receive not, because ye ask amiss."

—JAMES 4:3.

FROM the very beginning we approach prayer with a grave misconception. Our selfishness knows no bounds. In more or less naive self-love we look upon everything in our environment with which we come in contact as our agencies, as things which exist for our sakes, as something for us to make use of and utilize to our own advantage. We think and act as though everything, inanimate things, plants, animals, human beings, even our own souls, were created for the purpose of bringing gratification to our selfish desires.

And we make no exception of God.

As soon as we encounter Him, we immediately look upon Him as another means of gaining our own ends. Natural persons in their relation to God have this one purpose more or less consciously in mind: How can I, in the best way, make use of God for my own personal advantage? How can I make Him serve me best now, in the future and throughout all eternity?

Natural persons look upon prayer, too, in this light. How can I make use of prayer to the greatest possible advantage for myself? This is the reason why the natural person seldom finds that it pays to pray regularly to God. It requires too much effort, takes too much time and is on the whole impracticable, for the simple reason that one even forgets to pray.

But when these same persons get into trouble in one form or another and cannot help themselves or get help from anybody else, then they think that it might pay to pray to God. They then pray to Him incessantly, often crying aloud in their distress.

And when God does not put Himself at their disposal immediately and answer them, they are not only surprised, but disappointed and offended, deeply offended.

Why should there be a God, if He is not at the disposal of those who need Him? That God should exist for any other purpose than to satisfy people's selfish desires does not even occur to such people.

Many are they who after an experience of this kind are forever done with prayer. When you cannot get what you ask for, and in times of great need even ask for imploringly, why should you pray?

✠

It is not difficult for us, who have opened our hearts to the Spirit of prayer and have learned a little about prayer, to see that such people have misunderstood the meaning of prayer. The use to which they put prayer is wholly and completely a misuse of prayer. They pray in direct contravention of the very idea of prayer. That this does not lead to good results, but instead becomes a source of disappointment, as mentioned, is self-evident.

But it is not only the natural person who in this way misunderstands and misuses prayer. Unfortunately, many believers are often guilty of doing the same thing.

We, too, have a carnal nature; and when it can gain some advantage or be delivered from some great suffering or misfortune, it has no objections whatever to praying. On the contrary, then it, too, manifests a desire to pray which is nothing short of wonderful.

We should note well that the temptation to misuse prayer is native to us and comes, therefore, automatically to every believer.

In Matthew 20:20-23 we have a typical example of misunderstood, misused and unanswered prayer.

The sons of Zebedee came with their mother to Jesus one day and asked for the highest places of honor in the earthly kingdom which was about to be established, as they thought. Their prayer was no doubt offered in all innocence and good faith. They were cousins of Jesus and had, together with Peter, already been given positions of preference in the intimate circle of Jesus' friends. What they desired was that Jesus at this early hour should assure them of the leading positions in the kingdom also when it had reached its consummation.

Verse twenty-four says that when the other apostles heard what the two had done, they became indignant.

But Jesus reacted in an entirely different way. And that is what I wish to emphasize here. It is true, He replied immediately by saying explicitly that He could not comply with their request, but otherwise He took very kindly and understandingly to the whole affair. He advised them of their fault and explained everything to them. Such a tender and fervent tone runs through the whole admonition which Jesus gave them that it warms our very souls.

It tells us what Jesus' attitude is toward us when we come by families into His presence and ask Him to favor us in every possible way and avert from us all danger and all unpleasantness. He does not become angry with us as we might expect. He understands us, advises us of our mistakes and tells us how we should pray.

This is what the Spirit of prayer undertakes to do every time we misuse prayer and ask for things for ourselves, for our own enjoyment. Lovingly and kindly, but firmly, He reminds us that this is not in accordance with the true meaning of prayer. He shows us that this is to pray amiss, and points out our mistakes.

To begin with we do not understand what He means perhaps. All we experience is inner unrest, both while we pray and after we have prayed. Besides, of course, we notice that our prayer is not granted.

This is usually sufficient for honest souls. They begin to search themselves and to examine their prayers. This gives the Spirit of prayer an opportunity to gain a full hearing. They begin to see how they have misused prayer, how the words of James apply fittingly to many of their prayers: "Ye ask, and receive not, because ye ask amiss, that ye may spend it in your pleasures."

When such people begin to realize this, they become both amazed and alarmed to see to what an extent their zeal and their prayers for Christian enterprises are dependent upon the extent to which they themselves are connected with these enterprises.

If, for instance, there is to be a devotional meeting in their home, how earnestly and perseveringly they pray that the meeting may be richly blessed! But if a similar meeting is to be held in a neighbor's home, they do not always remember even to pray for the meeting.

Or, if they themselves are to preach, bear witness, or sing at a meeting, how they pray early and late for the meeting. But if they are not to speak, everything is altogether different both as far as intercession for the meeting and interest in it are concerned.

Or, if "their" organization is arranging for something, a Bible conference, or a mission meeting, for instance, then they are vitally interested, and then they pray faithfully for the event. But, on the other hand, they find that they are not a little less zealous and less diligent in prayer when some other organization is arranging similar events.

Or, it may be that an important matter is to be decided. They pray for God's guidance in arriving at a decision in accordance with His will. But they discover that their prayers after all were not concerned about ascertaining the will of God, but, on the contrary, about getting God's will and blessing to coincide with their own wills and purposes in the matter.

Whenever we have caught ourselves misusing prayer in this way a few times, we will agree fully with the words of James quoted above. And we will then feel more humble and helpless in our prayer life than ever before. We will realize how passionately selfish our own hearts are and how replete with egotism our whole prayer life has been. From the bottom of our hearts we will begin to cry, "Lord, teach me to pray!"

Whereupon the great change takes place in our prayer life. Having learned not to trust in ourselves, not even when we pray, we cling helplessly to the Spirit of prayer whenever we pray. And henceforth it is the desire of our hearts to be kept from profaning and misusing prayer.

The way is now open. Little by little the Spirit of prayer can now reveal to us the meaning of prayer and the ends toward which God would have us make use of prayer.

BOOK SEVEN

The Meaning of Prayer

> "And whatsoever ye shall ask in my name, that will I do, that the Father may be glorified in the Son."
>
> —JOHN 14:13.

ABOUT twenty years ago I made a fairly extended trip into Germany for the purpose of studying there. After having worked hard for some time, I had decided to take a little vacation. Accordingly, I planned a trip to Switzerland to pay a visit to the old patriarch, Samuel Zeller, in Männedorf. He conducted a "spiritual sanatorium" on the shores of Lake Zürich for people who desired rest, not only for their bodies, but also for their souls.

Zeller was an unusually gifted man, both by nature as well as by spiritual endowment. He was an excellent organizer and had succeeded in gradually building up a large institute for the care of people who were mentally or physically ill, tired, or worn out nervously.

He was an outstanding speaker. I have heard men with greater natural ability as speakers, but I have never heard anyone who has surpassed Zeller as a preacher. He succeeded in accomplishing what should be the real objective in all preaching: to bring the listeners into the presence of God by means of the Word. It was as though all else faded away and we stood in the presence of God alone when Zeller spoke.

He was exceptional also as a pastor. I, at least, have never met anyone in whom such a profound knowledge of human nature was coupled with such tender, sympathetic love.

Lastly, he had received the extraordinary gift of grace of healing by prayer. By the prayer of faith he was able to help a large number of people and set them free from many a physical and spiritual infirmity.

And yet none of these things made the deepest impression upon me. My strongest impression was that of Zeller in prayer.

I do not think that I exaggerate when I say that I have never heard anyone pray as he did, although I have heard many who were more emotional and more fervent when they prayed. Zeller, on the contrary, was quiet and confident while he prayed. He knew God well, and for that reason he was confident.

I do not believe that I have ever heard anyone expect so much of God and so little of his own prayers as he did. He merely told God what was needed. He knew that God would take care of the rest. His prayers were reverent, but natural, conversations with God, as though God were sitting in the first pew and Zeller were standing before Him.

Zeller had much to pray for when we assembled for morning devotionals. First, he prayed for our fellowship, then for the whole institution with all its aged and infirm patients, and finally for all the sick and unfortunate everywhere who had sent him letters asking for intercession. During the short time that I was there letters came to him from every country in Europe, with the exception of Norway and Sweden.

Thus he prayed every day for many people and for many things. But as I listened to these prayers of his I had to say to myself, "After all he prays only one prayer, namely, that the name of God might be glorified."

Oftentimes he prayed for miracles. But never without adding, "If it will glorify Thy name." Nor was he afraid to pray for instantaneous healing, but always with the provision mentioned above.

He made no attempt to dictate to God or to force Him by His own promises. Miracle-working prayer was not to Zeller a means of escaping tribulation; it was only a means of glorifying the name of God.

For that reason he would often say, "If it will glorify Thy name more, then let them remain sick; but, if that be Thy will, give them power to glorify Thy name through their illness."

And he did not only pray that way for others. He who had been instrumental in healing others, was himself afflicted with a dangerous internal ailment, which might at any time cause his own painful death. He knew that he was called to glorify God through his ailment.

✠

Here the purpose and meaning of prayer dawned upon me for the first time. Here I was privileged to see more clearly than ever before the purpose of prayer: to glorify the name of God.

The scales fell from my eyes. I saw in a new light the misuse of prayer and the difficulties connected with prayer as well as the place of our own efforts in prayer.

Prayer life has its own laws, as all the rest of life has. The fundamental law in prayer is this: Prayer is given and ordained for the purpose of glorifying God. Prayer is the appointed way of giving Jesus an opportunity to exercise His supernatural powers of salvation. And in so doing He desires to make use of us.

We should through prayer give Jesus the opportunity of gaining access to our souls, our bodies, our homes, our neighborhoods, our countries, to the whole world, to the fellowship of believers and to the unsaved.

If we will make use of prayer, not to wrest from God advantages for ourselves or our dear ones, or to escape from tribulations and difficulties, but to call down upon ourselves and others those things which will glorify the name of God, then we shall see the strongest and boldest promises of the Bible about prayer fulfilled also in our weak, little prayer life. Then we shall see such answers to prayer as we had never thought were possible.

It is written, "And this is the boldness which we have toward him, that, if we ask anything according to his will, he heareth us: and if we know that he heareth us whatsoever we ask, we know that we have the petitions which we ask of him" (1 John 5:14-15).

The apostle establishes the fact from his own prayer experience as well as that of his readers, that if we pray for anything according to the will of God, we already have what we pray for the moment we ask it. It is immediately sent from heaven on its way to us. We do not know exactly when it will arrive while we are asking for it; but those who have learned to know God through the Spirit of God, have learned to leave this in His hands, and to live just as happily whether the answer arrives immediately or later.

✠

By this time no doubt some of my sincere praying readers are feeling depressed. After what has been said so far, you are beginning to suspect that you have misunderstood and misused the sacred privilege of prayer altogether. You have in your daily prayer life been speaking with God about everything, about greater as well as lesser things. You have even asked Him for most insignificant things.

And you are afraid that this is a misuse of prayer, and that you should therefore cease at once. A deep sigh arises from your heart.

Nay, my friend, you should by no means cease. On the contrary, you should pray God for still greater simplicity of mind in your daily conversation with Him. Pray that you may become so confidential with Him that you can speak with Him about everything in your daily life. That is what He desires. That is just how He would have us pray. You will no doubt recall that it is written, "In nothing be anxious; but in everything by prayer and supplication with thanksgiving let your requests be made known unto God" (Philippians 4:6).

He knows that it is in our daily lives that we most easily become anxious. He knows, too, that our daily lives are made up of little things, not great things. Therefore He beckons to us in a friendly way and says, "Just bring all those little things to me; I am most willing to help you."

Be sure to remember that nothing in your daily life is so insignificant and so inconsequential that the Lord will not help you by answering your prayer. Some day you may perhaps be looking for some keys that you have lost. You must have them, and you are in a hurry, and you cannot find them. Go trustingly to God and tell Him about your predicament. Or, perhaps your little boy is out playing. You need him at once to run an errand for you. But you cannot take the time to look for him or to run the errand yourself. Tell it confidently to your Father in heaven.

Do not forget, however, what we mentioned above, that prayer is ordained for the purpose of glorifying the name of God. Therefore, whether you pray for big things or for little things, say to God, "If it will glorify Thy name, then grant my prayer and help me. But if it will not glorify Thy name, then let me remain in my predicament. And give me power to glorify Thy name in the situation in which I find myself."

Some may think that this will weaken the power and the intensity of our prayers. But this is due to a misunderstanding of prayer as a whole. To pray is to let Jesus come into our need. And only by praying in this way will we succeed in opening our hearts to Jesus. This will give Him the opportunity to exercise His power on our behalf, not only as He wills but also when He wills.

✠

Peace and tranquillity will then fill our hearts.

As mentioned above, restlessness in prayer comes from striving against the Spirit of prayer. But when we in prayer seek only the glorification of the name of God, then we are in complete harmony with the Spirit of prayer. Then our hearts are at rest both while we pray and after we have prayed. The reason is that we now seek by our prayers only that which will glorify the name of God.

Then we can wait for the Lord. We have learned to leave it to Him to decide what will best serve to glorify His name, either an immediate or a delayed answer to our prayer.

Permit me to cite an example to show how bold, even importunate, prayer can become when the one who is praying desires nothing but the glorification of the name of God by his supplications.

In 1540 Luther's good friend, Frederick Myconius, became deathly sick. He himself and others expected that he would die within a short time. One night he wrote with trembling hand a fond farewell to Luther, whom he loved very much.

When Luther received the letter, he sent back the following reply immediately, "I command thee in the name of God to live because I still have need of thee in the work of reforming the church. . . . The Lord will never let me hear that thou art dead, but will permit thee to survive me. For this I am praying, this is my will, and may my will be done, because I seek only to glorify the name of God."

Myconius had already lost the faculty of speech when Luther's letter came. But in a short time he was well again. And, true enough, survived Luther by two months!

Nothing makes us so bold in prayer as when we can look into the eye of God and say to Him, "Thou knowest that I am not praying for personal advantage, nor to avoid hardship, nor that my own will in any way should be done, but only for this, that Thy name might be glorified."

✠

If we pray in this way, we shall have peace of mind also when our petitions are not granted.

At this point let us say a few words about unanswered prayers.

It cannot be denied that they cause us all a great deal of difficulty, especially our children. They have been taught to pray to Jesus, and they have been told that He is kind and good, and that He helped all who came to Him when He lived here on earth below. As a result they pray confidently to Him for everything, large and small. And they expect in all sincerity to receive that for which they have prayed.

A great crisis enters into the life of the child. The child has prayed to Jesus for something, but has not received an answer to his prayer.

Here it is necessary for us to come to the assistance of the child and explain the situation. And in speaking with children we must speak graphically; otherwise they will not be able to understand us. We must illustrate by means of examples.

We can tell them, for instance, that we have read in the papers every now and then about children who have accidentally shot themselves either with an air rifle or an ordinary gun and have become cripples for life, and that sometimes children have even been killed in that way.

How did this happen?

Because they had asked their fathers and mothers for air rifles and because they were so unfortunate as to receive what they asked for. If only their fathers and mothers had had sense enough not to give them such dangerous weapons, they would have been spared the terrible misfortune.

This will teach the child that God is merciful even when He declines to give us things that we ask of Him.

As far as that is concerned, we need to learn this lesson over and over again, because we forget so easily. We have by nature a great deal of confidence in ourselves and think that we know best what is good for us. And when God thinks differently in the matter, we suspect immediately that He is not concerned about us.

Even the Great Apostle had experiences with unanswered prayers.

Paul tells us that on one occasion he prayed three times and still did not receive what he asked for (2 Corinthians 12:9-10). It was a question of an affliction which was apparently causing him a great deal of trouble in his missionary work. He prayed God to take it away from him. But God declined to heed his supplications.

This refusal was certainly not made because Paul had misused prayer by praying that the thorn in the flesh might depart from him merely in order that he might escape affliction. On the contrary, he prayed that the thorn might be removed for the sake of his missionary labors. The real purpose of his prayer was to glorify the name of God. Nevertheless his prayer was not granted.

When Paul in this case continued to pray three times, it must have been because he was conscious that he was praying, not for personal advantage, but for the glorification of the name of God.

When God nevertheless failed to heed his supplications, it was because His name would be glorified even more by having Paul keep his affliction. By so doing, Paul would be kept humble and receptive at all times to the power of God.

Through this prayer-struggle Paul learned the great secret of fellowship with God which he expresses thus: "When I am weak, then I am strong."

Even Jesus prayed a prayer which the Father did not fulfill; and He, too, prayed three times, "Father, if it is possible, let this cup pass away from me." That was in Gethsemane, when Satan by tempting Jesus was permitted to render obscure that which all the way had been clear to Jesus, that He must suffer and die in order to save the race.

But even in the dark hour of temptation we see the pure and obedient mind of Jesus. He tells His Father candidly how He feels in temptation's darkness. But the real desire of His prayer is nevertheless this: "Not as I will, but as thou wilt."

From this we learn that we should not be afraid, when praying to God, to give expression to a definite desire, even though we are in doubt at the time we are praying whether it is really the right thing to pray for or not.

Regardless of this, I say, we should pray for definite things, for those, namely, concerning which we feel a strong desire to speak to our heavenly Father. But at the same time we should do as Jesus did and add, "Nevertheless, not as I will, but as thou wilt."

BOOK EIGHT

Forms of Prayer

"Pour out your heart before him!"

—PSALM 62:8.

PRAYER is a part of our soul's life with God and is marked therefore by some of that manysidedness and indescribability which we find in life in general. This is also true of the forms of prayer, its expressions. As we have seen, this may vary from the quiet, meditative mood to that of energetic, even violent striving.

Prayer is, as shown above, a condition of mind, an attitude of heart, which God recognizes as prayer whether it manifests itself in quiet thinking, in sighing or in audible words.

Because prayer is an expression of our personal life with a personal God, it readily assumes the forms and characteristics of personal life. We know that conversation between persons does not take place according to certain prescribed rules and regulations, but occurs freely and spontaneously as the occasion may require. That is what makes conversation personal, gives it life and freshness. The more personal conversation is in this sense of the word, the more it becomes real communication, a mutual exchange of ideas in which life speaks to life.

So also with prayer.

It should be free, spontaneous, vital fellowship between the created person and the personal Creator, in which Life should touch life. The more that prayer becomes the untrammelled, free and natural expression of the desires of our hearts, the more real it becomes.

As a vital means of communication between the soul and God, prayer can assume very different forms, from quiet, blessed contemplation of God, in which eye meets eye in restful meditation, to deep sighs or sudden exclamations of wonder, joy, gratitude or adoration. It may take the form of one word, as when we cry, "God!" "Jesus!" Or it may take the form of a smooth, quiet conversation lasting for many minutes, perhaps even hours. Or it may be an outcry from a violently agitated soul engaged in a bitter struggle.

We can classify all of these forms of prayer, each of which is well adapted to some phase of the prayer life, under the following main headings:

1. Supplicatory Prayer.

By this we mean request prayer, the turning to God to receive something. Naturally, this aspect of prayer is always in the foreground. The word in the Scriptures which is most often used to designate prayer really means to express a desire.

There is something beautiful about this.

It is the will of our heavenly Father that we should come to Him freely and confidently and make known our desires to Him, just as we would have our children come freely and of their own accord and speak to us about the things they would like to have. And I hope to God that nothing I may have said in the foregoing will have obscured this gracious aspect of prayer.

It is written, "In everything by prayer and supplication with thanksgiving let your requests be made known unto God" (Philippians 4:6). Herein are included also those petitions which we afterwards may learn were misused prayers. Do not be so afraid, in other words, of misusing prayer that you on that account omit giving expression to the desires of your heart when standing in the presence of God.

We parents want our children to come to us with their desires. Then we can decide whether they can have them granted or not. And even though their requests must be denied many a time, nevertheless we want them to continue to come to us and speak to us about their wishes.

My praying friend, even though you have misused prayer often, continue nevertheless to make known your desires to God in all things. It is when we can speak with one another about anything and everything that conversation really affords us freedom and relief. Let Him decide whether you are to receive what you ask for or not.

If He cannot give it to you, He will do unto you as He did to the sons of Zebedee (Matthew 20:20-23) and to Paul (2 Corinthians 12:7-10). He will speak with you tenderly and sympathetically about the matter until you yourself understand that He cannot grant your prayer.

By so doing you will learn three good things: God's deep and far-sighted solicitude for you, your own lack of wisdom and your selfishness in prayer, but also the unlimited freedom which is yours to give expression in prayer to all the desires of your heart.

2. The Prayer of Thanksgiving.

This follows naturally upon supplicatory prayer. Having received something from God, it is self-evident that we ought to return thanks to Him for it.

The Scriptures contain a number of both direct and indirect admonitions to give thanks to God. The strongest one is found in Ephesians 5:20, "Giving thanks always for all things in the name of our Lord Jesus Christ."

That is what God means by the prayer of thanksgiving. From this we learn, too, that giving thanks should constitute a very essential part of prayer.

This is, however, a very difficult type of prayer. It is hard for us to learn to pray, but it is still harder to learn to give thanks.

Notice our own children! We do not need to teach them to pray for the things they desire. But what untiring efforts does it not involve to train them to say, Thank you!

It is easy for us to think that God is so great and so highly exalted that it does not make any difference to Him whether we give thanks or not. It is, therefore, necessary for us to catch a vision of the heart of God. His is the most tender and most sensitive heart of all. Nothing is so small or inconsequential that it does not register an impression with Him, whether it be good or bad. Jesus says that He will not forget even a cup of cold water if it is given in grateful love of Him.

How much Jesus appreciates gratitude can be seen very clearly from the account of the ten lepers whom He restored to health (Luke 17:11-19). He had healed them by sending them to the priests to receive the certificate required by law to show that they had been cleansed of their leprosy. While they were on their way to the priests, they were suddenly cleansed, every one of them. Nine of them continued on their way to receive their certificates. And in so doing they were in reality complying with Jesus' words, "Go and show yourselves unto the priests."

One of them, however, turned about, went back to Jesus joyfully speaking His praises, fell down on his face before the Lord and returned thanks to Him.

Notice the impression it made upon Jesus. Listen to the tone in His query, "Were not the ten cleansed? But where are the nine? Were there none found that returned to give glory to God, save this stranger?"

Here we are also told by Jesus Himself that to give thanks means to give glory to God. This explains why it is so blessed to give thanks. Even though our efforts to thank

God in prayer are weak, nevertheless we find that when we succeed in truly thanking God, we feel good at heart. The reason is that we have been created to give glory to God, now and forevermore. And every time we do so, we feel that we are in harmony with His plans and purposes for our lives. Then we are truly in our element. That is why it is so blessed.

It is not only blessed to give thanks; it is also of vital importance to our prayer life in general. If we have noted the Lord's answers to our prayers and thanked Him for what we have received of Him, then it becomes easier for us, and we get more courage, to pray for more. It is no doubt right to begin our prayers with thanksgiving.

This is especially fitting because we receive, according to the Scriptures, "exceeding abundantly above all that we ask or think" (Ephesians 3:20). We neither know of all the things we need each day, nor do we have the will to pray for them. But God gives them to us nevertheless. What gratitude this should awaken in our hearts!

If you are as ungrateful as I often am, my friend, I would pass this advice on to you: begin by giving thanks to God for the temporal gifts you have received from Him, such as physical health, the use of your mental faculties, strength for your daily tasks, the desire to work, house and home, food and clothing and the dear ones whom you love and who love you. Begin with these things and you will notice that it will become easier for you to see and to give thanks for the spiritual gifts which the Lord has showered upon you.

If someone has rendered a great service to you or your dear ones in a difficult situation, then you feel the desire to meet that person, grip his or her hand fervently and say from the bottom of your heart: "Thank you very much for what you have done for us."

My friend, do the same to Jesus.

He is not made of stone. He is moved to happiness every time He sees that you appreciate what He has done for you. Grip His pierced hand and say to Him, "I thank Thee, Savior, because Thou hast died for me." Thank Him likewise for all the other blessings He has showered upon you from day to day.

Do this often during the day, in the midst of your work as well as when you are resting. It brings joy to Jesus. And you yourself will become glad.

3. Praise.

Even in the Old Covenant they had learned to praise the Lord. In fact, the saints of God in the Old Dispensation had progressed far in the art of praising God. This comes to light especially in the Psalms. Not a small portion of the Book of Psalms is made up of songs of praise, praise to God. And in a large number of the remaining psalms we find that a doxology is used either at the beginning or at the close of the psalm.

"Praise is comely for the upright" (33:1).

"Bless Jehovah, O my soul,
And all that is within me, bless his holy name" (103:1).

"While I live will I praise Jehovah" (146:2).

"I will bless Jehovah at all times" (34:2).

"Oh, magnify Jehovah with me,
And let us exalt his name together" (34:3).

"Praise him according to his excellent greatness" (150:2).

Praise and thanksgiving are very closely akin to each other. Outwardly it is not possible to draw a clear line of demarcation between them. Both consist in giving glory to God.

From ancient times, however, people have tried to differentiate between them by saying that when we give thanks we give God the glory for what He has done for us, and when we worship or give praise, we give God glory for what He is in Himself.

In that event, praise lies upon a higher plane than thanksgiving. When I give thanks, my thoughts still circle about myself to some extent. But in praise my soul ascends to self-forgetting adoration, seeing and praising only the majesty and power of God, His grace and redemption.

But inasmuch as we experience the majesty and the grace of God only as He has revealed Himself in acts of merciful kindness toward us, we can readily understand that praise and thanksgiving will overlap and complement each other. Thanksgiving will naturally express itself in praise. And praises will be called forth by the acts of merciful kindness for which we are giving thanks.

From Jesus' lips we hear words of praise on two occasions. On the one we hear His own soul's blessed adoration of the Father, "I praise thee, O Father, Lord of heaven and earth, that thou didst hide these things from the wise and understanding, and didst reveal them unto babes: yea, Father, for so it was well-pleasing in thy sight" (Matthew 11:25-26).

On the second occasion He taught us to bring our prayers to a close with the words, "For thine is the kingdom, and the power, and the glory for ever and ever, Amen" (Matthew 6:13).

In the New Covenant the songs of praise center about God's greatest revelation of grace, the giving of His own Son to suffer and die for our sins. "God be praised for his unspeakable gift!" (2 Corinthians 9:15).

In the Revelation of John we learn that songs of praise shall resound throughout the heavens in all eternity. And the theme of the eternal song of praise is stated briefly as follows:

"And every created thing which is in the heaven, and on the earth, and under the earth, and on the sea, and all things that are in them, heard I saying,

"Unto him that sitteth on the throne, and unto the Lamb, be the blessing, and the honor, and the glory, and the dominion, for ever and ever" (Revelation 5:13).

In heaven the song of praise will be perfect. There God will be given the glory which belongs to Him. There the songs of praise shall resound everywhere and be re-echoed by everybody. There we shall all be as harps in tune, which, with individual variations, and yet in perfect symphony, will make melody unto Him.

Our songs of praise here on earth are imperfect as everything else here below. Nevertheless, no one can become a member of the celestial choir who has not learned to sing His praises here below. "He hath put a new song in my mouth, even praise unto our God" (Psalm 40:3). And He would have us learn to sing this song with greater purity of tone and greater frequency, the more we experience His unspeakable gift.

The apostle admonishes us to praise God individually as well as collectively: "speaking one to another in psalms and hymns and spiritual songs, singing and making melody with your heart to the Lord" (Ephesians 5:19 and Colossians 3:16).

As far as I am able to observe, we praise God very little individually or collectively. It appears from our old hymns that it was easier for our Christian forbears to sing praises than it is for us.

Let us begin to make more frequent use of the powerful hymns of praise which our ancestors sang when we assemble for worship. They will lift our hearts from the valleys of beggary and complaint up to the eternal peaks, where we can gain a true perspective from which to view our experiences in life, our adversity as well as our prosperity. After having sung praises with the words of others for a time, we shall soon learn to praise God in our own words. We shall learn to "make melody in our hearts unto the Lord."

4. Conversation.

If prayer, as mentioned above, is the natural form of communication between the soul and God, it is also evident that it includes conversation.

Conversation is the free and natural exchange of ideas between persons. The wider the range of subjects included in their conversation, the richer their fellowship.

To pray is to let Jesus into our lives.

He knocks and seeks admittance, not only in the solemn hours of secret prayer when you bend the knee or fold your hands in supplication or when you hold fellowship with other Christians in a prayer meeting; nay, He knocks and seeks admittance into your life in the midst of your daily work, your daily struggles, your daily "grind."

That is when you need Him most.

And He is always trying to come into your life, to sup with you. He sees that you need His refreshing presence most of all in the midst of your daily struggles.

Listen, therefore, to Jesus as He knocks in the midst of your daily work or rest. Give heed when the Spirit beckons you to look to Him in silent supplication, He who follows you day and night.

There is more to prayer than asking.

He who has given us the privilege of prayer never tires of us, even though we never do anything else when we pray than to ask of Him. But He does desire to teach us also to converse with Him in prayer.

Since children came into our home I have understood this better than before. They come to me with all their failures. And they have wonderful faith in the ability of their father to make everything right again. If their playmates have things which they themselves do not have, they come in and ask for these things too.

This is wonderful, even though I cannot make good all their failures and still less give them everything they ask for. But there is something which gladdens my heart even more. That is when they come rushing in, the one falling over the other, to tell me something that they have experienced. At times they become so enthusiastic that they all talk at once in order to get it told as quickly as possible.

God is glad in a similar way when we, His little children, feel a desire to speak with Him about our daily experiences.

He desires to share with you the little things of life. That is always the way when two people love each other. They share everything, little things as well as big things, their joys as well as their sorrows. That is what makes love so rich and so joyous.

Speak, therefore, with God about your daily experiences. They need not be great or important. Speak with Him about the little things which make up your daily life. Tell God when you are happy. Let Him share your joy. That is what He is waiting to do.

Tell God when you are sad, when you are worried, when you do not know what to do, when you are anxious. He is waiting to hear about it because He loves you. This being the case, nothing is inconsequential or unimportant. Everything that concerns you interests Him.

God never intended that we should live our Christian life in any other way. Everyday Christianity cannot be practiced unless we incessantly receive into our lives that supply of spiritual power which is necessary in order to preserve within us that spirit which is willing to deny self, to serve others, to endure wrong and to let others have the last word.

Furthermore, God desires to be with us in all of our daily struggles. He desires to help us and make even our purely temporal tasks easier. So completely does He give Himself to us. He desires to share everything with us.

This is the best part of our whole Christian life.

Nothing is so blessed as quiet, unbroken communication with our Lord. The sense of the Lord's nearness, which then fills our souls, is greater than any other peace, joy, inner satisfaction, or security which we have known. Even adversity and sorrow lose their sting when we share everything with the Lord. Lina Sandell has expressed this with depth and beauty in the following lines:

> "A little while with Jesus—
> Oh, how it soothes the soul,
> And gathers all the threads of life
> Into a perfect whole."*

Everything is different when the Lord is at our side. Our work becomes easier. Our difficulties no longer frighten us. Not even human contrariness or the unpleasantness we experience at the hands of others can disturb our peace. In the quiet, peaceful joy which we are experiencing we do not feel like being angry with them; we feel more like embracing them and saying to them, "You can be as mean as you like; that does not matter as far as I am concerned; I am happy in the Lord."

Only they succeed in living a peaceful, victorious, happy Christian life who have learned the profound secret of daily renewal: to turn to God incessantly for a new and fresh supply of power from the realms of eternity.

That most of us live a weak Christian life is due without question to the fact that this part of our prayer life is not in order.

Prayer is the breath of the soul.

Our breathing is a constant source of renewal to our bodies. We eat three or four times a day. But we breathe all day long, all night too.

As impossible as it is for us to take a breath in the morning large enough to last us until noon, so impossible is it to

---

*Translation by N. N. Rønning.

pray in the morning in such a way as to last us until noon. Therefore, too, the apostle says, "Pray without ceasing" (1 Thessalonians 5:17). Let your prayers ascend to Him constantly, audibly or silently, as circumstances throughout the day permit.

✠

5. Prayer Without Words.

As we have seen above, prayer is really an attitude of our hearts toward God. As such it finds expression, at times in words and at times without words, precisely as when two people love each other. As conscious personalities we must and should give expression to our attitudes in words one to another. It is this faculty which lifts the fellowship of human beings to such a high plane and makes it so rich.

But at the same time let us remind ourselves that life, in the last analysis, is inexpressible. There is something in our lives, also in our fellowships, which can never be formulated in words, but which can be the common experience, nevertheless, of two who share with each other everything that can be expressed in words.

In the soul's fellowship with God in prayer, too, there are things which can and should be formulated in words. We have spoken of that in the preceding. But there are also things for which we can find no words. Likely it is this to which the apostle makes reference when he speaks in Romans 8:26 of the "groanings which cannot be uttered."

My little boy came in one day and stuck his little head into the doorway of my study. Now he knew that he was not supposed to disturb me during working hours. And his conscience troubled him a little on account of this. But he looked at me nevertheless with his kind, round baby eyes and said, "Papa, dear, I will sit still all the time if you will only let me be here with you!"

That he received permission when he approached my father-heart in that way, every father knows.

That little experience gave me a great deal to think about.

Is not that just the way we often feel with regard to our heavenly Father? We do so love to be with Him, just to be in His presence! Moreover, we never disturb Him, no matter when we come nor how often we come!

We pray to God. We speak to Him about everything we have on our minds both concerning others and ourselves. There come times, not so seldom with me at least, when I have nothing more to tell God. If I were to continue to pray in words, I would have to repeat what I have already said. At such times it is wonderful to say to God, "May I be in Thy presence, Lord? I have nothing more to say to Thee, but I do love to be in Thy presence."

We can spend time in silence together with people whom we know real well. That we cannot do with others. We must converse with them, entertain them either with interesting or profound things as the case may be. But with our own dear ones we can speak freely about common and insignificant things. In their presence, too, we can be silent.

It is not necessary to maintain a conversation when we are in the presence of God. We can come into His presence and rest our weary souls in quiet contemplation of Him. Our groanings, which cannot be uttered, rise to Him and tell Him better than words how dependent we are upon Him.

As evening drew nigh, and our little fellow had played until he was tired, I noticed that he drew closer and closer to his mother. At last he found the place he was longing for, mother's lap. He did not have a great deal to say then either. He simply lay there, and let his mother caress him into sleep.

We, too, become tired, deathly tired, of ourselves, of others, of the world, of life, of everything! Then it is blessed to know of a place where we can lay our tired head and heart, our heavenly Father's arms, and say to Him, "I can do no more. And I have nothing to tell you. May I lie here a while and rest? Everything will soon be well again if I can only rest in your arms a while."

We will all have use for wordless prayer, if not before, when the death-struggle and the death-agony tax all our energies. That does not always take place exactly at the moment of death. The death-struggle is usually fought out some time before the end comes.

I have witnessed the death-struggle of some of my Christian friends. Pain has coursed through their bodies and souls. But this was not their worst experience. I have seen them gaze at me anxiously and ask, "What will become of me when I am no longer able to think a sustained thought—nor pray to God?"

If they only realized what they were doing, the people who postpone conversion until they become ill! My friend, in the death-struggle your physical and mental energies will all be taxed to their utmost by your suffering and pain. Remember that and repent now, the acceptable time.

When I stand at the bedside of friends who are struggling with death, it is blessed to be able to say to them, "Do not worry about the prayers that you cannot pray. You yourself are a prayer to God at this moment. All that is within you cries out to Him. And He hears all the pleas that your suffering soul and body are making to Him with groanings which cannot be uttered. But if you should have an occasional restful moment, thank God that you already have been reconciled to Him, and that you are now resting in the everlasting arms."

BOOK NINE

Problems of Prayer

"If ye have faith as a grain of mustard seed, ye shall say unto this mountain, Remove hence to yonder place; and it shall remove; and nothing shall be impossible unto you."

—MATTHEW 17:20.

LIFE is full of problems. It is, therefore, not strange that the prayer life, too, has its problems. Let me briefly mention some of them.

1. How can prayer accomplish such tremendously great things when in itself it is so weak?

To superficial minds this question may seem quite superfluous. It is written, they say, that if we have faith, we can remove mountains. Everything, therefore, depends upon faith. Our prayers are effective when we are strong in faith. And when we are not strong in faith, our prayers lose their effectiveness.

Yes, to some it seems as easy as that.

But people who have had a somewhat wider experience in the remarkable realm of prayer will not accept this as the final solution of the problem. Of course, they know that great and wonderful results often take place after people have prayed with great faith. There are times when the Spirit of prayer whispers into our hearts, "Ask for it, and you shall receive it," and when we are fully assured even before we have finished praying that we shall receive the wonderful answer we are seeking.

But as a rule it does not work out as beautifully as that. On the contrary, many have received the most remarkable answers to prayer when they have had no clear or definite assurance that they would be heard either before they prayed, while they prayed or after they prayed. It has seemed to them as though God has given them the mightiest and most remarkable answers to prayer at times when they have had no faith whatsoever.

Such things are not published in the papers, but wonderful things are nevertheless experienced in all quietude in the family circle of the Lord's humble friends. Praise the Lord!

People who have had experiences such as this in prayer are often in a quandary and ask, "How can prayer accomplish such wondrously great things when it is so weak in itself?"

The solution of this problem lies in the very nature of prayer itself.

To pray is nothing more involved than to let Jesus come into our hearts, to give Him access with all His power to our needs. From this it is clear that success in prayer does not depend upon the assurance of the people praying, nor upon their boldness, nor any such thing, but upon this one thing, that they open their hearts to Jesus.

And this is, as we have seen before, not a question of *power* but of *will*. Will I have Jesus come in to my need?

But this depends again on how helpless I am. Prayer is a mysterious instrumentality and can, in the final analysis, be employed to full effect and with perfect success only by those who are helpless.

Using an illustration from everyday life, we may compare prayer to an electric wiring system. The electric current is available, but it must be turned on. For that purpose we have what is known as a switch. All we need to do is to move the switch slightly, and the electric current flashes through the whole house. And we know, of course, that not much power is required to turn on a switch.

When humanity fell into sin, our souls were not only cut off from God, but the whole wiring system was destroyed. To restore it, Jesus had to suffer and die. The wiring is now in order again. We may all re-establish contact with, and make use of, the powers of the heavenly world. And prayer is the mysterious little instrumentality whereby the contact is made, enabling the powers of His salvation to reach our souls and our bodies, and, through us, to others, as far as our zeal and perseverance will permit.

2. Why should we pray?

To many this problem, too, seems easy to solve. We should pray, they say, in order to get God to give us something!

So simple does it appear to them.

But a moment's reflection will convince us that this view of prayer is pagan and not Christian. We all have so much of the pagan left in us that it is easy for us to look upon prayer as a means whereby we can make God kind and good, and grant our prayer. But the whole revelation of God teaches us that this is to misunderstand both God and prayer completely.

God is in Himself good, from eternity and to eternity; He was good before humanity had any occasion for prayer. The Scriptures also teach us that God is equally kind and good whether He grants our prayers or not. When He grants our prayers, it is because He loves us. When He does not, it is also because He loves us.

Others say, "No, the purpose of prayer is to tell God what we need."

But neither is this solution adequate to the problem involved in Christian prayer. By the revelation of God we Christians are convinced that as far as God is concerned it is not at all necessary for us to explain our needs to Him. On the contrary, God alone fully understands what each one of us needs; we make mistakes continually and pray for things which would be harmful to us if we received them. Afterwards we see our mistakes and realize that God is good and wise in not giving us these things, even though we plead ever so earnestly for them.

But this again throws us into a quandary as to why we should pray at all.

If God gives us His gifts of His own accord, and if He does not need to be told by us what to give, why should we pray at all?

This question is not one of mere theoretical interest. It is one of great practical importance because of the way it affects our views both of God and of prayer. The question is in reality this: Why does not God give us His gifts before we pray, even without our prayer, since He is Himself good, and since it is His will to give us these things, and since He does not need any suggestions from us?

In answering this question, we must take as our starting point the words of Jesus in Matthew 5:45, "He maketh his sun to rise on the evil and on the good, and sendeth rain on the just and on the unjust." In these words Jesus reveals clearly that aspect of God's perfect love according to which He gives everybody all that He can persuade them, in one way or another, to accept.

"On the evil and on the good," says Jesus. The evil do not ask Him for it, but He gives it to them nevertheless. The good ask, to be sure; but if they did not receive more than they prayed for, they would not receive very much. Hence both have this in common, that they receive a great deal from God without asking for it.

Why do they receive these things without asking?

Simply because God is love. And *the essence of love is to give:* give all it has to give, give all it can give without bringing harm to the loved one, give all it can persuade the loved one to accept.

That God gives some gifts to people without their prayer and other gifts only to those who pray, can be accounted for by the simple fact that there is a wide difference in kind between these gifts.

All people accept some of God's gifts; this is true, for instance, of temporal gifts. They are given without our prayer.

But we close our hearts to some of God's other gifts; this is true of all the gifts which pertain to our salvation. These gifts God cannot bestow upon us before He can persuade us to open our hearts and receive them voluntarily. And, as we have seen above, prayer is the organ whereby we open our hearts to God and let Him enter in.

Here we see why prayer is essential.

It is not for the purpose of making God good or generous. He is that from all eternity.

Nor is it for the purpose of informing God concerning our needs. He knows what they are better than we do. Nor is it for the purpose of bringing God's gifts down from heaven to us. It is He who bestows the gifts, and by knocking at the door of our hearts, He reminds us that He desires to impart them to us.

No, prayer has one function, and that is to answer "Yes," when He knocks, to open the soul and give Him the opportunity to bring us the answer.

This throws light on the struggles and strivings, the work and the fasting connected with prayer. All these things have but one purpose: to induce us to open our hearts and to receive all that Jesus is willing to give, to put away all those things which would distract us and prevent us from hearing Jesus knock, that is, from hearing the Spirit of prayer when He tries to tell us what God is waiting to give us if we will only ask for it.

3. Does God need our intercessory prayers?

Here, assuredly, we touch the greatest problem in the whole realm of prayer.

We have just seen that prayer is essential to personal friendship with God. But now we come to intercessory prayer. And we ask: Are our intercessions necessary as far as God is concerned and the work He would have accomplished in this world?

Nor is this problem one of mere theoretical interest; it, too, is one of practical significance because of the manner in which it affects our view of God, of prayer and of the world.

We can answer by saying, in the first place, that it is impossible for God to bring the world forward to its goal without humankind.

The attitude which we take is the vital factor in determining whether the world shall attain its goal or not. God has voluntarily bound Himself to us in His government of the world. From the very beginning of the history of revelation we see that God has established His kingdom only where He could find people who would voluntarily permit themselves to be used by Him.

It thus becomes evident that God has voluntarily made Himself dependent also upon our prayer. For, after all, prayer is the deciding factor in the life of all who surrender themselves to God to be used by Him.

What we do in God's kingdom is entirely dependent upon what we are. And what we are, depends again upon what we receive. And what we receive, depends again upon prayer. This applies not only to the work of God in us, but also to the work of God through us.

I shall mention in this connection only this one word of Jesus, "The harvest truly is plenteous, but the laborers are few. Pray ye therefore the Lord of the harvest, that he send forth laborers into his harvest" (Matthew 9:37-38). Here Jesus says that it is God who must send forth the workers, but also that He is dependent upon our prayer. He does it through our prayer.

In this passage, Jesus flashes a remarkable gleam of light upon God's relation to the world and our intercessions.

We know that only by an uninterrupted influx of eternal, soul-saving power into the world can the race be created anew and brought into the kingdom of God. These saving powers are contained in the person of Jesus Christ. But they must be transmitted from Him to human beings. And God has so ordained it that this transmission of power takes place through those who accept salvation, and thus open their hearts to the saving power of Jesus.

In the Old Covenant there were only a few through whom He could transmit this power. Since the day of Pentecost this has been changed. Now He makes use of all who accept salvation. Let us note that every believer represents a daily influx into this world of eternity's powers of salvation. The supernatural influence of God's Spirit upon a believer's personal life results in an accession of eternal power which manifests itself in various ways in his or her environment and quietly but surely helps to transform this world into God's kingdom.

The greatest transmission of power takes place through the believer's prayers and intercessions. Believing prayer is unquestionably the means by which God, in the quickest way, would be able to give to the world those saving powers from the realm of eternity which are necessary before Christ can return and the millennium be ushered in.

When will the Church of God awaken to her responsibility?

In prayer the Church has received power to rule the world. The Church is always the little flock. But if it would stand together on its knees, it would dominate world politics—from the prayer room.

And the result would be one of two things, either a world-wide revival or the appearance of Antichrist.

4. Are prayer and answers to prayer consistent with God's government of the world?

From the Scriptures and from our own experience we are certain that prayer changes things with respect to the way God governs, not only individuals, but society, the nations and the whole world.

Therefore many ask, "Can God really rule the world according to a definite plan and toward a definite goal if a single individual can persuade Him to change His plans merely by asking Him to do so? Would this not lead to utter chaos? One might pray for rain; another, for sunshine; another, for wind; and another, for calm weather."

To this we must reply that God has never intended that prayer should be used in that way.

In the first place, God has not promised to answer the prayers of everybody, only the prayers of His children and the prayers of those who pray that they might become His children.

In the second place, He has not even promised to answer all the prayers of His children, only those which are prayed in the name of Jesus, or, as is written elsewhere, "If we ask anything according to his will, he heareth us" (John 5:14).

In these words Jesus has designated the extent to which we by our prayers can affect the divine economy and has pointed out that only those prayers can have any influence which are wrought by the Spirit of Christ in the hearts of believers and which, therefore, look toward the realization of His kingdom-plans.

When God changes the divine world-economy as a result of our prayers, we mean that He governs the world with such a degree of elasticity that He can alter His methods as circumstances here below require, be they good or bad. He does not alter His kingdom-plans, only the means and methods whereby He at each moment seeks to accomplish them. God takes immediate cognizance, therefore, of our prayer in His government of the world. Something does take place as a result of our prayer, which otherwise would not take place. In fact, as we have just seen, our prayer is one of the most effective means by which God directs the world forward towards its goal, the Kingdom of God.

5. Does God also answer the prayers of the unconverted?

This question, too, has more than a theoretical interest. It has great practical significance for the unconverted who have experienced definite and immediate answers to prayer, and who accept this as a proof that they are children of God.

To others, such answers to prayer are a deep and profound mystery. They themselves have experienced such answers to prayer while still unconverted. After their conversion they began to worry about this. They began to ask themselves, "Does it make any difference to the Lord whether someone who prays is converted or not?" As they grew more and more skeptical, they asked themselves, "What, after all, is prayer, if unconverted people, too, receive what they ask for?"

In answering this question, I would say, first, that the Lord has not promised to hear the prayers of any but His own regenerate children. It is to them that the promises have been given.

But God has the privilege of doing more than He has promised. He can, of course, as often as He wills to do so, grant also the prayers of unconverted people. That God has done this, the Scriptures tell us very plainly in Genesis 4:13-16. Here we are told that God heard the prayer of Cain though he was not in the least repentant and turned to God only because he was afraid of the consequences of his sin.

Why does God at times grant the petitions even of unconverted people?

Several reasons might be mentioned. I shall, however, confine myself to those nearest at hand. God, at times, grants the prayers of the unconverted for the same reason that He showers other blessings upon them, namely, because He loves them and desires to save them. Answer to prayer becomes one of the gracious means whereby God seeks to bring such people to repentance.

I know personally of people who have been converted and saved through such answers to prayer. But I also know of some who, like Cain, have been strengthened in impenitence by such answers. But this is the law of God's salvation, either acceptance or rejection.

BOOK TEN

The School of Prayer

"Lord, teach us to pray."

—LUKE 11:1.

NOW do you dare to pray, "Lord, teach me to pray"? That is right, be honest. You are afraid of trials and afflictions. And I believe that both you and I are willing to admit that we are also afraid of God. Pure instinct seems to tell us that God is going to deal harshly with us. And the same instinct seems to tell us that we can rely on ourselves, and that we understand what is good and what is not.

But remember one thing, neither you nor I will be happy before we yield ourselves to His pierced hands and say to Him:

> Send me e'en where death defies me,
> Send me where oppression tries me,
> Through dark storms upon life's sea!
> As Thou wilt, beloved Savior,
> If but Thou wilt show Thy favor,
> Constantly my staff to be.*

By so doing you will be enrolling voluntarily in that school of prayer which the Spirit has established for such as do not know how to pray.

So few of us become sanctified and skilled petitioners because we do not continue in the school of prayer. The course is not an easy one, and the difficulties do not consist

---

*Translation by P. A. Sveeggen.

alone in the temporal and spiritual trials mentioned above. There is something about this school which tries our patience sorely. Jesus Himself alludes to it on several occasions, especially in Luke 18:1-8, where He says "that they ought always to pray and not to faint."

We become faint very easily. How many times have we not earnestly resolved in our own minds to pray for certain people and for certain causes, only to find ourselves growing faint. We were not willing to expend the effort. And little by little we ceased to intercede for others.

It is the Spirit of prayer who superintends the instruction in the school of prayer. He does not offer a variety of subjects, but concentrates purposely on a few central things. It is not necessary to master a large variety of subjects in order to become skilled in prayer. I would mention briefly only the following:

In the first place, the Spirit must be given an opportunity to reveal Christ to us every day. This is absolutely essential. Christ is such that we need only "see" Him, and prayer will rise from our hearts. Voluntary prayer, confident prayer. We know that Christ can answer prayer. We know also that it gives Him joy to do so. Prayer and intercession have become a delightful and fascinating means of cooperation between Christ and the praying soul.

The instruction which the Spirit imparts has as its aim the removal of everything which hinders Him from revealing Christ in our hearts. We have spoken of this previously in the chapter on "Wrestling in Prayer."

In the second place, the instruction which the Spirit imparts aims at making us earnestly solicitous.

Intercessory prayer is like an ellipse, which rotates about two definite points: Christ and our need. The work of the Spirit in connection with prayer is to show us both, not merely theoretically, but practically, making them vital to us from day to day.

Comfort yourself with the thought that it is the Spirit who is working these things in your heart every day. It is not necessary for you to strive in your own strength to keep your eyes open to Christ and the needs of the world.

No, all you need to do is to listen to the Spirit as He speaks to you every day in the Word and through prayer about Christ and your need, and you will soon notice yourself making progress both in prayer and in intercession.

In the third place, the Spirit teaches us the necessity of self-denial in connection with prayer.

There is something about prayer and intercession which calls for more self-denial than any other work to which the Spirit calls us. The greater part of the work of intercession is, of course, done in secret; and work of this kind requires the expenditure of greater effort than work which can be seen of others. It is astonishing to see how much it means to us to have others see what we do. It is not only that we all have a great weakness for the praise of others, but the fact that our work is appreciated and valued is a remarkable stimulant to us.

Furthermore, we all love to see results from our labors. But the work of prayer is of such a nature that it is impossible for us always to know definitely whether what happens is a fruit of our own intercession or that of others.

Both of these facts call for a great deal of self-denial in connection with prayer.

That is why it is difficult for the Lord to get enough people to carry on this work. It is easy enough to get people to preach. Many are anxious to preach and are offended if not asked to do so. And we who are asked to do so, are so zealous that when we once get into the pulpit it is difficult to get us out again. But there are not many who are willing to take upon themselves the self-denying work connected with prayer, because it is neither seen nor appreciated by others.

You may perhaps have prayed for some unconverted people in your neighborhood, perhaps for many years. Then a revival starts in your neighborhood, and the first ones to be converted are the very ones for whom you have been praying so faithfully. No one besides yourself, however, knows anything about that. You have kept it, as is right and proper, a secret between yourself and God. Consequently, no one talks about what you have been doing. But the name of the preacher who has spoken at the meetings is, on the other hand, on everybody's lips. All are loud in their praises of him and say, "My, what a great evangelist!"

My friend, when you begin to grow tired of the quiet, unnoticed work of praying, then remember that He who seeth in secret shall reward you openly. He has heard your prayers, and He knows exactly what you have accomplished by means of them, for the salvation of souls. If not before, then on the Great Day, you will come bringing in the sheaves, the fruit of your labors.

In the fine and difficult art of prayer, intercession is undoubtedly the most difficult of accomplishment. As far as my understanding of these things goes, intercessory prayer is the finest and most exacting kind of work that it is possible for people to perform.

But it is also the most important work, as we have shown in the chapter, "Prayer as Work."

None of us who had visited the institution in Männedorf, mentioned above, doubted that Zeller was the leading man and the one upon whom the greatest responsibility rested for that great and varied work which was being done there. Zeller seemed to sense our feelings in this matter, so he told us one day about the one who was chiefly responsible for and the main factor in the whole work. It was an old woman who, together with one Miss Trudel, had been connected with the work from the very beginning. During that whole time she had persevered humbly in intercessory prayer. Now she was so old and weak that she was confined to her bed. But Zeller told us, with tears in his eyes, how she had literally lived in prayer and faithfully carried her coworkers to God on the arms of prayer from day to day.

Since intercessory prayer is such a fine and difficult art, it is not at all remarkable that it should require a long and rigorous period of training. It is true that the Lord leads His friends in various ways. And we must take care not to lay down rules for Him. But what we ourselves have seen, we need not be afraid to mention. As for me, I must say: The best and most faithful intercessors I have met learned the holy art of intercession only after many trials or great suffering. All that some of them could do at last was to lie in bed, scarcely able to whisk a fly away from their faces, like the woman in Männedorf of whom I have spoken.

But how they could pray!

Though they lay unseen by others, nevertheless they were centers of spiritual power, and by their simple and persevering prayers they were the chief supporters of the Christian work which was being done in their neighborhood, their community, their country and even to the ends of the earth.

Every time I meet one of these unseen intercessors, I am reminded of a great electric power plant. They, too, are often hidden away in some secluded valley. But they are, nevertheless, exceedingly important, a fact which we become aware of especially when they do not function. When that happens, our homes are darkened and our factories brought to a standstill.

✠

One of the tenants on my father's farm was one of these faithful intercessors.

His name was Jørn. Our Lord had imposed severe limitations upon him from his birth. His eyes were weak, and as a result it was always difficult for him to earn a living. But he did fairly well nevertheless. According to good Haugean custom, Christian people saw to it that no brother or sister need go to the poor commissioner. Trials and tribulations became Jørn's lot, and many a day was dark and dreary.

But he humbled himself beneath the mighty hand of God, and little by little, in the school of difficult experiences, he learned the holy art of prayer. He would pray for his home community day and night. And, in due time, God exalted him. He became the spiritual counsellor of the whole parish. People came to his little hut from the whole vicinity to get advice and help. And if Jørn could not help them in any other way, he could give them some of the unfeigned love of his own tender heart. Besides, he prayed for them; and as the years passed, many a soul left his humble dwelling with a lighter tread and a happier heart.

In the later years of his life he was very poorly. Two elderly Christian women, who were with him and cared for him, told me that he would be awake a great deal at night, and that, while thus awake, they could hear him pray for all the people of the parish. And he did not make as light of it as we are apt to do. As a rule we are always in a hurry, so we take them all in one group to the Lord and ask Him in one prayer to bless them all.

But old Jørn didn't do it that way. He mentioned each one of them by name, as in his thoughts he went from house to house. Even children whom he had not seen, but who he knew had been born, he felt that he had to carry to the throne of grace upon the arms of prayer.

How much such people do mean to us! How empty their places become when they are gone!

There was also something remarkable about the way Jørn left us. Everyone thought that his passing would be like a beautiful ascension, and believers vied with one another for the privilege of being with him and watching over him; but our Lord very neatly foiled them in the expectations they had set for themselves. Jørn died without anybody witnessing his death; the one who happened to be watching over him was out in the kitchen to get something when it happened.

Jørn's funeral was the largest ever held in my home community. He had no relatives there, having moved into the parish; but people came from the whole neighborhood. And they stood at his casket and wept as though they had lost a father. Even ungodly people, who had never cared to hear the Word of God, came to his funeral; and they, too, wept.

Even in death, Jørn was a blessing to others. Both his life and his death were a fulfillment of the words of Scripture, "Ask, and ye shall receive."

BOOK ELEVEN

The Spirit of Prayer

"And I will pour upon the house of David, and upon the inhabitants of Jerusalem, the spirit of grace and of supplication."

—ZECHARIAH 12:10.

"We know not how to pray as we ought; but the Spirit himself maketh intercession for us with groanings which cannot be uttered."

—ROMANS 8:26.

THROUGHOUT this whole book I have spoken of the Spirit of prayer. My desire has been that this thought should be the red thread running through every chapter and binding together into a unified whole the various things I have said about prayer.

In conclusion, may I try to sum up everything I have said under the one heading, The Spirit of Prayer. What I wish to emphasize before I bring these meditations to a close is that the Spirit of prayer throws light upon every phase of our prayer life.

From this vantage point we can see light falling upon every detail of the prayer life. Not only theoretical light, enlightening our minds, but practical light for our use in praying and for our training in prayer.

My praying friend, who, like myself, must admit that you as yet are not very well acquainted in the realm of prayer, do pray a little each day in a childlike way for the Spirit of prayer; and you will have some wonderful experiences in this realm, which has so many surprising things in store for you.

If you feel that you know, as yet, very little concerning the deep things of prayer and what prayer really is, then pray for the Spirit of prayer. There is nothing He would rather do than unveil to you the grace of prayer.

If you find the difficulties in prayer so insurmountably great that you become disheartened, then pray for the Spirit of prayer. He will help you in your weakness and show you in what ways you misunderstand prayer, and will make it simple and easy for you to pray.

If the work of prayer becomes burdensome to you, and you feel your heart becoming weary of praying, then pray with childlike simplicity for the Spirit of prayer. It is written that the Lord will pour out the Spirit of prayer. You need not then work yourself up into the spirit and attitude of prayer.

If wrestling in prayer becomes a hard and bitter struggle, and you feel that your soul is out of touch and tune with God, and your prayers only empty words, then pray trustingly for the Spirit of prayer. He will point out the sin which is acting as a hindrance to your prayers and will help you to acknowledge it. And then He will make Christ so precious to you that you will voluntarily give up that sin which is threatening to sever your connection with God.

If you notice that you have been inclined toward the misuse of prayer, to selfish and self-indulgent prayer, and you scarcely have the courage to pray any more, then pray again for the Spirit of prayer. He will not only show you the true meaning and purpose of prayer; He will also lift you in all your helplessness up to the very heart of God where you will again be warmed by His love, so that you can again begin to pray according to His will, asking for nothing except those things which are in harmony with His plans and purposes.

If you are scarcely able to pray, still less able to give thanks, and least of all to worship and praise Him, then pray for the Spirit of prayer. There is nothing He would more gladly do than teach you these things.

If the problems of prayer have become so dark and heavy to you that the words of prayer freeze on your lips, then pray in your distress for the Spirit of prayer. He will solve the deepest mysteries of prayer by revealing to you that, the more helpless you are, the better you are fitted to pray, and the more answers to prayer you will experience.

And if the school of prayer becomes tedious and tiresome to you, then speak to the Spirit of prayer about this too. He is doing the teaching Himself, and He will see to it that it becomes neither more tedious nor more tiresome than you can endure. Now and then He will give you a little recess. He knows what we are made of and remembers that we are dust.

✠

Such childlike petitions for the Spirit of prayer will little by little bring about a change in our prayer life which we hardly thought possible.

Without noticing it ourselves, prayer will become the great centralizing and unifying factor in our distracted and busy lives. In everything that we experience during the day, our minds and our hearts will quietly and naturally be drawn toward God. A longing to talk with God about everything else will arise. Everything we see and hear in connection with our dear ones, our friends, our enemies, the converted or the unconverted, temporal or spiritual affairs, small things and great, the hard and the easy, all the observations and experiences which fill and shape our daily lives, will naturally and readily begin to take the form of prayer. Intimate friends tell each other of their experiences as soon as possible. So it is in prayer, too. The Spirit of prayer makes us so intimate with God that we scarcely pass through an experience before we speak to Him about it, either in supplication, in sighing, in pouring out our woes before Him, in fervent requests, or in thanksgiving and adoration.

You will experience sweet release in thus speaking with God about everything in your daily life and especially while it is fresh in your mind and of actual interest to you. By so doing you will be able to lay aside your cares and responsibilities and leave everything in God's hands.

You will begin to realize more and more that prayer is the most important thing you do; and that you can use your time to no better advantage than to pray whenever you have an opportunity to do so, either alone or with others, while at work, while at rest, or while walking down the street. Anywhere!

We can make use of our time in no better way.

Let us then make use of prayer! Put in your applications for help to Him who ruleth on High whenever you or your dear ones are in need of anything—or someone else that you meet during the day. Do not delay, send them off at once. And write on all of them, "Grant them only if they will glorify Thy name!"

Send your applications for help by the wireless telegraphy of prayer. On high they will be carefully noted and tabulated, and in God's own time the answers will come back to you. The more completely you cease being concerned about the time in which your prayers are to be answered, the more freedom you will enjoy in your prayer life.

The things you will now see will surprise you!

The longer you live a life of this kind, the more answers to prayer you will experience. As white snow flakes fall quietly and thickly on a winter day, answers to prayer will settle down upon you at every step you take, even to your dying day. The story of your life will be the story of prayer and answers to prayer.

It is written, "Goodness and mercy shall follow me all the days of my life" (Psalm 23:6). Verily the answers to your prayers will follow you, and none of them will fail to reach their destination. They are yours from the very moment you begin to pray in the name of Jesus, but they do not all reach you just as quickly. And when you have prayed, it is not any more necessary for you to exert yourself to receive answers to your prayers than it is to exert yourself to receive letters which have been addressed to you. They are brought by our efficient postal system directly to our doors.

This shower of answers to prayer will continue to your dying hour.

Nor will it cease then. And when you pass out from beneath the shower, your dear ones will step into it. Every prayer and every sigh which you have uttered for them and their future welfare will, in God's time, descend upon them as a gentle rain of answers to prayer.

Our family has been a believing and praying family for three generations. The elders have prayed faithfully for their descendants. During my whole life I have walked in the prayers of my parents and forbears and in the answers to these prayers. A quiet rain drips steadily down upon me. I reap, in truth, what others have sown.

My friend, if you are not able to leave your children a legacy in the form of money or goods, do not worry about that. And do not wear yourself to death either physically or spiritually in order to accumulate a great deal of property for your children; but see to it, night and day, that you pray for them. Then you will leave them a great legacy of answers to prayer, which will follow them all the days of their life. Then you may calmly and with a good conscience depart from them, even though you may not leave them a great deal of material wealth.

He who thus provides for his whole future life by childlike, persevering prayer will experience answers to prayer: not only in life, but also in death.

Make your hour of departure a subject of prayer. Pray frequently about it. Pray like the aged countess did:

> "My God, wilt Thou for Christ's dear sake
> My hour of parting peaceful make!"*

My father used to tell about a Christian woman that he knew.

She was unmarried and had no near relatives. When old age began to make its appearance, she went one day to one of her neighbors, a well-to-do Christian farmer, and said to him, "I have $1,200. Will you in return for it take me into your home and care for me until I die?"

"No," he said, "that might become too expensive an affair. You may be sick a long time, and that may make it difficult for us."

"But I am not going to be sick," she said.

To which he replied, "Neither you nor I know anything about that."

Then she looked him steadily in the eye and answered, "Yes, I do know. I have asked God not to let me become ill."

This did not, however, convince him; and she had to go elsewhere. Accordingly, she went to another Christian farmer in the neighborhood with the same proposal, and he received her into his house.

She lived many years, enjoying excellent physical health and leading a fervent spiritual life, a blessing to the whole household. She did her share of work every day and did her part at the spinning wheel as faithfully as any of the other women.

One morning she did not come in for breakfast as usual. Immediately they went to look for her, and found her dead

*Translation by P. A. Sveeggen.

in bed, without a sign of a struggle on her face. Altogether without pain the Lord had taken her while she slept. Her prayer had been heard.

She had not become ill. The evening before she had been well and happy as usual.

Why had she prayed that she might escape sickness?

Was it in order to evade suffering? No, it was to spare the good people who might take her into their home the trouble which her illness would entail.

This little incident has been of great comfort and help to me.

It has taught me to pray about my death. Not only that I might die saved through the blood of Christ, but also that I might glorify God by my death; and that my dear ones might be left behind with the full assurance that I died as a sinner saved by grace.

Let us blend our voices with the unknown poet and all the many unknown Christians who with him have sung and prayed:

"Though I'm but dust, I pray,
Before God standing,
Not asking pleasure's way,
Nor gold demanding;
But greater things I ask,
From God requesting
No less than that He give
To me that I may live
Life everlasting."*

And now, finally, if it becomes difficult for you to pray, then offer this little prayer, "Lord, teach me to pray." There is nothing that He, the Spirit of prayer, would rather do.

*Translation by P. A. Sveeggen.

"My heart now overflows
With prayers and praises.
My Heavenly Father knows
Each sigh that raises
My heart ever nearer His heart
so tender;
For there's my joy and peace;
In Thee I've found release,
My soul's Defender."*

*Translation by P. A. Sveeggen.

✠

STUDY GUIDE

SOMETIMES IT'S GOOD to take a friend along on the most ordinary and common experiences to gain a different, and often helpful, perspective. The purpose of this study guide is to help you discover different and helpful perspectives on Ole Hallesby's book, *Prayer,* so that your prayer life may be encouraged and enhanced.

This study guide has eleven chapters, corresponding to Hallesby's eleven chapters (he calls them "books"). In each chapter of this guide you will be challenged to REACT to Hallesby's writing. REACT is an acronym for **R**eview, **E**xamine, **A**pply, **C**ompare, and **T**hink.

REVIEW	To review Hallesby's chapter by recalling major principles or ideas.
EXAMINE	To examine what Hallesby wrote through critical thinking and questioning.
APPLY	To apply the principles of the chapter to one's life.
COMPARE	To compare the principles of the chapter with biblical examples and instruction.
THINK	To think more deeply and in different ways about the content of Hallesby's chapter. This may be viewed as "extra" study for the serious student.

Whether you use this guide individually or in a group, a few general hints may be helpful. First, when examining the subject of prayer it is a good practice to have your Bible close at hand. Second, take your time; sometimes we read too much and think too little about what we read. Third, attempt to strike a healthy balance between what you understand in your mind and what you practice with your behavior; in Christian experience, knowledge and action are inseparable. And fourth, pray as you go through the process of learning more about prayer!

One of the ways to understand and appreciate Hallesby's book is by understanding and appreciating his life.

About Ole Hallesby

Ole Kristian Hallesby was born in Norway in 1879. He was the son of a farmer and grew up in a Lutheran church that emphasized the Bible and a conservative life-style. Although for a time he adopted a more liberal theological position, he returned to the faith and piety of his youth.

In his twenties he was ordained, served as an itinerant preacher, and studied in Germany. He acquired his doctorate in Berlin and around the age of thirty was appointed professor of systematic theology at the Free Faculty of Theology in Norway. For more than forty years he lectured and became a spiritual leader and teacher to a generation of Norwegian pastors. During World War II, because of his leadership in the church's opposition to Nazi Germany, he was arrested and placed in a concentration camp until the end of the war.

Hallesby wrote many devotional books, among them *Prayer* in 1931, *Why I Am a Christian* in 1930, and *Under His Wings* in 1932. He also wrote theological textbooks: *Christian Dogmatics* and *Christian Ethics* were written in the 1920s. Many of his books have been translated into other languages, and his personal travels led him to the Scandinavian countries, Iceland, and the United States. In 1947 he became the first president of the International Fellowship of Evangelical Students. He died in 1961.

1

What Prayer Is

Review

Hallesby's first chapter deals with "What Prayer Is," an appropriate place for any book on prayer to begin. You cannot understand what a car is by simply reading an instruction manual. To really understand what a car is you must experience the car by driving it. Prayer, too, must be experienced. Understanding prayer is both an intellectual and experiential endeavor. Prayer is for both the mind and the heart.

Prayer is communicating with God, but who takes the initiative? The answer, according to Hallesby, is Jesus, who is always knocking at the door of your heart, inviting you into the experience of prayer.

Reread the first three paragraphs of Hallesby's first chapter to help you prepare for a more thorough examination of his perspective on the nature of prayer.

Examine

1. Read Revelation 3:20. Recall Hallesby's definition of prayer, which is based on this verse. What is your reaction to this definition?

2. Have you ever felt or believed that prayer starts with our moving Jesus to listen to our prayers? How might our perspective on prayer be changed with the understanding that it is Jesus who moves us to pray?

3. Hallesby writes that "All He [Jesus] needs is access" (p. 14). What may be some of the reasons why people would either deny Jesus access into their hearts or not even hear Him knocking at the door of their hearts? What are some of the consequences of not hearing or responding to the knock of Jesus?

4. What are the two attitudes of the heart that God recognizes as prayer? How can the first attitude of the heart prepare a person for developing the second attitude of the heart? Are there any attitudes that are natural extensions or outcomes of the second attitude?

5. Why could a person feel that a proper attitude of prayer would be strength, as opposed to helplessness? What are the differences between these two attitudes and the possible results of having such attitudes? What do you think Hallesby's view would be in this regard?

6. How are the attitudes of helplessness and faith central to the entire Christian life and not just to the prayer life?

7. According to Hallesby, "The essence of faith is to come to Christ" (p. 30). Often faith in prayer can be taken to mean asking for a specific answer to a specific need and believing God will answer in that specific way. How is Hallesby's view of faith different? How can Hallesby's view be freeing to anyone who is helpless in attitude, in a situation, or both?

APPLY

8. How can the following contribute to developing an attitude of helplessness and faith in prayer: silence, stillness, journal writing, consistent Bible reading and study, praying with another person or a group? What are some of the other ways to develop and nurture these attitudes? Which one may be the most effective for you to try?

9. What do you feel helpless about in your own life? Do you feel spiritually helpless? emotionally helpless? physically helpless? Do you feel helpless about a situation or relationship? What would Jesus want you to do with your helplessness?

10. Do you presently approach prayer more with an attitude of helplessness or of strength? If from strength, what are your reasons? How does this approach hinder or conflict with the approach of helplessness?

11. Write a prayer that invites Jesus to come into your helplessness. Keep in mind that Jesus is already knocking at your heart's door.

Compare

12. Read Hebrews 11. What is the definition of faith found in 11:1? How does this compare with and complement Hallesby's definition?

13. Take a look at the testimony of Noah, Abraham, and Moses in Hebrews 11. Their faith is mentioned, but not any of their helplessness.
Compare the situations of Noah, Abraham, and Moses. They each were given tremendous promises or commands that may have been hard to believe or obey. Why did each of them have reason to feel helpless? Compare their responses to their seemingly helpless situations and how they each came to a place of faith. See Noah in Genesis 6, Abraham in Genesis 15:1-6, and Moses in Exodus 3:1—4:17.

Think

14. It may be easy to have an attitude of helplessness when things in life are not going well. How could you maintain this attitude of helplessness when things are going well?

15. The Bible speaks not only of helplessness, but of power. Think more about how helplessness and power can coexist. For further study look at Romans 8:37-39 and 2 Corinthians 12:7-10.

16. Read Revelation 3:1-22. Why is the church at Laodicea in a helpless situation? What does Christ call them to do in faith?

2

Difficulties in Prayer

Review

Prayer, according to Hallesby, is opening the door of one's heart to Jesus. The premise of Hallesby's second chapter is that the door of our heart does not always swing open so easily. This second chapter addresses common difficulties in prayer that can be overcome through practice and perseverance.

In the first chapter Hallesby states that helplessness and faith are the two attitudes of the heart that God recognizes as prayer. All that Hallesby develops can be traced back to these two necessary attitudes of the heart.

Examine

1. Take another look at the following verses with which Hallesby begins the chapter: John 15:5 Matthew 7:7-11 John 15:7 Philippians 4:6. Why does he begin with these verses? If we do not follow the instructions in these verses, why would we inevitably have difficulty in prayer?

2. Hallesby writes that, "He [Jesus] has all that we need." Consider this statement coupled with the opening verse of this chapter, 1 Corinthians 1:30. If Jesus has all we need, what does this verse tell us Jesus has? Look up the key words in this verse in a Bible dictionary to gain a better insight into their meaning.

3. What does 1 Corinthians 1:30 express about the purpose of prayer? How can knowing the purpose of prayer help someone identify difficulties in prayer?

4. What is your reaction to the following statement by Hallesby? "Prayer is a fine, delicate instrument. To use it right is a great art, a holy art" (p. 42).

5. One of the common mistakes in prayer is thinking we must help God fulfill our prayer. How could such a mistake be the result of having too low a view of God or too high a view of ourselves? What is a proper view of God? A proper view of ourselves?
6. Read the account of the wedding feast at Cana in John 2:1-11. How does Mary's attitude reflect both helplessness and faith? What is the significance of what Mary says and does not say? What do you learn through Mary's example?
7. Hallesby writes, "To pray in the name of Jesus is, in all likelihood, the deepest mystery in prayer" (p. 57). How can praying in the name of Jesus represent both a mystery *and* a way to clarify the purpose and practice of prayer?

APPLY

8. Of the three difficulties in prayer mentioned under "Review," which one do you most identify as a difficulty in your own prayer life? Is your difficulty the result of an improper attitude, lack of understanding, or a neglect of something you already know? Is there an area of your prayer life, other than one of these three, that is more of a difficulty for you?
9. Do you ever find prayer to be an effort? Do you look forward to private or group prayer? What do you think God's reaction would be if you told him right now how you feel about praying?
10. Choose one idea from the following list, or think of one yourself, that would help you overcome a specific difficulty you experience in prayer:
    - Begin each time of prayer this week by telling God how you honestly feel about praying.
    - In prayer, tell Jesus what you and others lack without

suggesting any solutions.

• Begin reading the Book of Psalms to expand your view of God.

• Commit to memory Ephesians 3:20-21.

• Start your prayers with "in Jesus' name," especially if you usually state that at the end.

• Write out one prayer each day for one week.

Compare

11. Read Matthew 6:5-13. What does Jesus value in prayer? What difficulty in prayer does he address?

12. Read the prayer of King Jehoshaphat in 2 Chronicles 20:6-12. Identify what is good about his attitude and his prayer.

Think

13. Hallesby makes the point that prayer is simply telling Jesus what we and others lack. When, if ever, is it appropriate not only to tell Jesus what we lack, but to tell him how we would like him to answer our prayer? Read and reflect on James 1:5-8, 5:17-18. For additional help see 1 Kings 18:16-39.

14. Prayer is a discipline that many people struggle with. Is there such a thing as a healthy and consistent struggle, even when a person avoids the common mistakes or difficulties Hallesby mentions? If so, describe this healthy struggle.

3

Prayer As Work

Review

Work, according to the Bible, is accomplished because God gives his energy and power to the task. If God does the work, what is the role and responsibility of the Christian? Hallesby's response is very clear: The work of the Christian is to pray. And prayer's basic and necessary attitude is that of helplessness and faith.

Our work is to seek the assistance of God; God's work is to accomplish the work. Our work is to acknowledge our helplessness; God's work is to be the Helper. Our work is to be open to God's work in our lives; God's work is to work within and around us to fulfill his purposes.

Hallesby insists that God has called us to superhuman tasks. But he who called us is faithful to equip us for the task with his Holy Spirit and with prayer.

Examine

1. Hallesby begins the chapter with a verse from the ninth chapter of Matthew. Read Matthew 9:35-38 to get the greater context of that verse. What might have been some other possible responses of Jesus after seeing the crowds? What is the wisdom behind Jesus' actual response?

2. The power of prayer, according to Hallesby, is mobile, independent of space and time, and not accessible to any of Jesus' enemies. Does this change any perspective on the people or things you are praying for?

3. "Prayer is the most important work in the kingdom of God" (p. 70). What is your reaction to Hallesby's words?

4. In the second part of this chapter are comments regarding the practice of one's prayer life. What are three specific

suggestions Hallesby makes? What would be some of the benefits of creating order and discipline in one's prayer life?

APPLY

5. Answer the following questions to gain some insight into the present role and place of prayer in your own life. Keep in mind there are no right answers!
   - For whom and what are you regularly praying?
   - When you spend time in prayer, do you wonder whom or what to pray for?
   - Do you ever spend time in prayer when you are all alone, quiet, still, and relaxed?
   - Do you pray regularly with any other person or group?
   - Do you pray often during the day? What prompts you to pray?
   - Are you satisfied with the quality of your prayer life? If not, what is missing?

6. Read Matthew 18:19-20. According to this passage, what are some of the benefits of praying with another person? What significance does the phrase "in my name" have for people who come together to pray? If you do not pray regularly with someone, why not? Do you know of a person you would like to pray with on a regular basis?

7. Hallesby mentions a number of people and causes that Christians need to remember in prayer. Make a list of these people and things. Add any other people or situations that are important to you. Don't forget personal concerns as well.

8. Using six days of the week, or some other workable pattern for you, devise a plan whereby you can pray for those people and things on a regular basis. Pray through the list once or twice (don't worry if it takes one day or

twenty days) and revise the plan to fit you and your needs.

Compare

9. Read 1 Corinthians 3:5-9 and Ephesians 2:10. Though these passages do not specifically deal with prayer, how do they relate to Hallesby's comments regarding prayer as work?

10. Jesus was asked the question, "What must we do to do the works God requires?" His response, in John 6:29, is: "The work of God is this: to believe in the one he has sent." What are the implications of Jesus' statement that the work is really to believe? Consider this in light of the second attitude of the heart that constitutes prayer, which is faith.

Think

11. Read Acts 1–2. Make a list of what God did and another list of what the Christians did. How did the experience of the first Christians correspond to what Hallesby writes about in this chapter?

12. What is the role and place of prayer in the church you attend? Talk to a pastor or church leader about their view of prayer in the church. What is one way you could more effectively pray for your church?

13. Reread Matthew 9:35-38. After Jesus saw the crowds he had compassion on them. After that He did not pray for the crowds, go to the crowds, or even send his disciples to the crowds. Why?

14. Which is more important: to pray for the unsaved or for Christian workers? Is a prayer for Christian workers also a prayer for the unsaved? Why or why not?

4

Wrestling in Prayer I

Review

Hallesby's comments on wrestling in prayer ring true for most people as they reflect upon their own experience in prayer. The adversary, Satan, is present to discourage, disrupt, and destroy the vital link of prayer in one's relationship with God. But Christians need to remember that God has given his Spirit for overcoming Satan and living a more abundant life, and this includes prayer. The responsibility of those who pray in Jesus' name is to yield to the Spirit who will do the wrestling for them. The promise for those who pray is that God will be faithful and do more than we ask or imagine as we yield to his Spirit.

Examine

1. Hallesby says that prayer is "the central function of the new life of faith" (p. 89). Why is it central and how does it function?

2. Why does Satan attack Christians when they pray? Why are his attacks often, as Hallesby points out, subtle, painless, and quiet?

3. Hallesby begins this chapter with the verse, "Watch and pray, so that you will not fall into temptation" (Mark 14:38). Reflect on the significance of the words "watch" and "temptation."

4. How does our aversion and disinclination to pray reaffirm the premise that our attitude in prayer needs to be one of helplessness and faith?

Apply

5. When you begin to pray, do you ever experience distractions? Do the distractions come from the world

around you or from within you? As you pray, do the distractions become greater or lesser? Why?

6. Do you have a specific time and place where you can pray undisturbed each day? If not, where and when could you pray?

7. Hallesby mentions that the "only way in which we can gather and keep collected our distracted minds and our roaming thoughts is to center them on Jesus Christ" (p. 93). List four truths or insights on prayer you have learned from Hallesby's book thus far that will help you center your mind and thoughts on Jesus Christ as you pray.

8. Another way to keep your mind and thoughts focused in prayer is to keep a journal on a regular basis. In the journal keep a record of who and what to pray about. Although devising a workable pattern of prayer was suggested in the previous chapter, consider the following more detailed pattern for weekly prayer:
   Every day—yourself, immediate family
   Monday—other family and friends, missionaries
   Tuesday—other family and friends, work, neighbors
   Wednesday—other family and friends, Christian leaders
   Thursday—other family and friends, government
   Friday—other family and friends, your church and community
   Saturday—important decisions regarding your life and future, preparation for Sunday worship and fellowship
   Sunday—thanks and praises, preparation for the week ahead

9. Complete the following statements:
   The next time I am distracted in prayer I will remember to ________________.
   The next time I don't feel like praying I will ______.

10. Memorize Philippians 4:4-7 and Romans 8:26-27.

Compare

11. Read Ephesians 6:10-18. How do Paul's insights agree with and enrich Hallesby's comments?

12. Read Luke 22:39-46. Compare the role of the angel in Jesus' experience to the role of the Holy Spirit in the Christian's experience. What does it mean to "pray more earnestly" (v. 44)?

Think

13. Hallesby makes the case for spending time in prayer. How would you respond to a person who says, "I can't spend a large quantity of time in prayer, but the time I do spend in prayer is quality time." What are some of the benefits of spending large quantities of time in prayer, even if that happens infrequently?

14. Read Psalm 139. Verse 7 states that the Spirit knows all about us and our lives. If we are aware that the Spirit knows us intimately, can this increase our willingness to yield to him as we pray? (See also Romans 8:26-27.)

5

Wrestling in Prayer II

Review

In this chapter Hallesby discusses striving in prayer and then fasting as they relate to wrestling in prayer. This chapter reads quickly and is fairly simple to comprehend. But don't be fooled! The deep things of God often veil themselves in simplicity.

Our responsibility is to be faithful to what we have learned and begin to put it into practice. As we do this, God will continue to deepen and expand our understanding and awareness of prayer.

Examine

1. According to Hallesby what does and does not constitute genuine striving in prayer? How is one's understanding of God's nature important in understanding what striving in prayer is?
2. Read the biblical accounts Hallesby mentions:
   The Canaanite Woman, Matthew 15:21-28
   The Death of Lazarus, John 11:1-44
   Jacob Wrestles with God, Genesis 32:22-32
   The Parable of the Persistent Widow, Luke 18:1-8
   Which passage most vividly displays striving in prayer for you? Why?
3. Discuss what it means to strive with self as opposed to striving with God. What is the role of the Holy Spirit in our striving in prayer?
4. Define fasting and its purpose. What are the circumstances in which one might feel the need to fast?

Apply

5. What was your understanding of striving in prayer before reading this chapter? How has your understanding been changed or enhanced?

6. Have you ever felt as if you have been striving with God? Why might this have happened?

7. Take a quick inventory of a few things you have been praying for that have not been answered (or at least not in the way you would like or anticipate). Reflect upon those prayer concerns in light of the following statement by Hallesby: "But if He had given us the things we prayed for immediately, He would not have succeeded in giving us what He had appointed for us" (p. 106).

8. What has been your understanding of fasting? How has this chapter changed or expanded your understanding?

9. What is one temptation or decision you currently face? Choose a day and time to fast over one of these concerns. (Keep in mind that the most important aspect of fasting to God is not the length, but the attitude of the heart. If this is your first time fasting, you may want to fast from one meal rather than for an entire day. And if you have any health concerns, be sure to contact your doctor.)

Compare

10. Read Ephesians 3:14-21. How does this passage accentuate Hallesby's comments? Consider memorizing verses 20-21.

11. Psalm 37:4 says: "Delight yourself in the LORD and he will give you the desires of your heart."
    Hallesby states that the "Spirit of prayer will put into our hearts the various things for which we should pray" (p. 112). How does the above verse fit with what Hallesby says and what, according to the verse, must one do to be given these desires? Read Psalm 37:1-7 to get a fuller appreciation for what the psalmist is saying and how it relates to Hallesby's comments.

Think

12. What might happen to someone who prays consistently but with a wrong understanding of the nature of God?
13. Do you sincerely believe God wants to bless you abundantly? Why or why not? Is your answer based on your understanding of God's nature or your own experience?
14. Consider Jesus' experience of, and teaching on, fasting. See Matthew 4:2-11; 6:16-18; 9:14-17; Luke 18:9-14.

6

The Misuse of Prayer

Review

The misuse of prayer will never result in effective prayer. Why? Because God knows the heart and mind of the one praying. And God alone answers prayer. Prayer has a proper use, and when we use it as God intends, God will reward us.

Prayer was designed for the very opposite thing our natural human nature tries to use it for. We try to use it for our ends and self-gratification, but God designed prayer for his glorification. And we, as God's children, can reflect his glory (2 Corinthians 3:18).

Examine

1. Hallesby identifies many ways in which prayer can be used selfishly. What are some of these ways?
2. Look up the words "carnal" and "natural" in the dictionary. How do their definitions add to your understanding of how we can misuse prayer?
3. What relationship is there between the reasons for the misuse of prayer identified in this chapter, and the attitude of helplessness that God recognizes as prayer, mentioned throughout earlier chapters?
4. What was Jesus' response to those who misused prayer?

Apply

5. After reading this chapter did you sense any ways in which you misuse prayer?
6. Hallesby mentions "inner unrest" as the result of misusing prayer. Is "inner unrest" something you can identify with?

7. The next time you find yourself misusing prayer, what could be a positive way to correct yourself?

Compare

8. Read Matthew 6:1-8. How are giving and praying misused? What is Jesus' response to this? See the first line of Matthew 6:9.

Think

9. Read Hebrews 4:14-16. How can a person pray with both selflessness and confidence?
10. Read 1 Corinthians 2:6-16 to gain a broader understanding of how the Spirit works in us to help us avoid the misuse of prayer. How can knowing the things of God prepare us for using prayer rightly?

7

The Meaning of Prayer

Review

Hallesby's experience with Samuel Zeller helped him discover the meaning of prayer. This took place after Hallesby had been a Christian. Therefore, Hallesby learned the true meaning of prayer after he had been praying, perhaps for years. This suggests that the meaning of prayer is discovered not before one prays, but after one begins. It is in the midst of prayer and praying, perhaps for years, that one discovers the deeper meaning of prayer, which is to glorify the name of God.

Examine

1. Look up the words "glory" and "glorify" in a dictionary. What does it mean to glorify God?
2. What is it about prayer that glorifies God? What role do God, Jesus, the Holy Spirit, and the one praying play in fulfilling the meaning of prayer?
3. What do rest, patience, and peace mean? Why will rest, patience, and peace be the *natural* result of someone glorifying God through prayer?
4. What is it about Jesus' experience in Gethsemane that makes it a perfect example to include in this chapter?

Apply

5. Do you regularly pray with the thought, "If it will glorify thy name"? Why or why not? What is one specific concern that you can pray about with the attitude, "If it will glorify thy name"? What difference will praying in this way make?

6. Can you think of a prayer concern for which you have prayed a long time? How does this statement by Hallesby relate to your experience: "If we pray for anything according to the will of God, we already have what we pray for the moment we ask it. It is immediately sent from heaven on its way to us. We do not know exactly when it will arrive" (p. 130).
7. Do you ever differentiate between big and little things to pray for? What is God's perspective on what is "little" or "big"? How might your perspective be changed to be like God's? Also, do you ever convey to others what is, in your opinion, a big or little thing to pray for? What message does this send to children or adults?

Compare

8. Read the Lord's Prayer in Matthew 6: 9-13. How does this prayer glorify the name of God?
9. Shortly before Jesus died he prayed to his Father in heaven. Read the first part of that prayer in John 17:1-5, looking for the words "glory" and "glorify." How does Jesus use these words? What does his use add to our understanding of the meaning of prayer?
10. Read Hebrews 1:3. How does this verse clarify your understanding of the meaning of prayer?

Think

11. Why is knowing God's will important in relation to praying, "If it will glorify thy name"? How can one know God's will?
12. Why does God want to have himself glorified? What happens to Christians when God is glorified?

8

Forms of Prayer

Review

In this chapter Hallesby describes five forms of prayer. Such forms need not be restrictive. They can help unite the one praying with God.

A key statement regarding the proper use of forms in prayer is this:

> Prayer is the breath of the soul. Our breathing is a constant source of renewal to our bodies. We eat three or four times a day. But we breathe all day long, all night too (p. 147).

Prayer is the natural result of living in relationship to Jesus. We can pray at specific times and in structured ways. But the goal is for prayer to become as natural as breathing.

Examine

1. List the five forms of prayer mentioned by Hallesby. Briefly explain them in your own words.
2. A number of times Hallesby uses the word "soul." Look up the word in a dictionary or Bible dictionary. See also Genesis 2:7 and Psalm 103:1-2 to gain further insight.
3. Why is there a need for many forms of prayer? What must be one's attitude in order for prayer to take place, regardless of what form the person uses?
4. Why is Hallesby's emphasis on helplessness and faith important to remember in understanding this chapter?

Apply

5. What forms of prayer do you use most often? Do you feel that your prayer life is routine or predictable? Does routine help or hurt your prayer life, or both?

6. Which one form of prayer that Hallesby mentions is most new to you? How can you incorporate this form into your prayer life this week?

7. Consider the following statement by Hallesby:

   We know that conversation between persons does not take place according to certain prescribed rules and regulations, but occurs freely and spontaneously as the occasion may require. So also with prayer (p. 137).

   What is the relationship between spontaneous and regular times of prayer? What has been your experience and what changes, if any, would you like to make in your own prayer life in this respect?

8. How might the truth that you are a *child* of God going to your Father in prayer change or renew your prayer life?

9. If you shared everything with God in prayer how might this change your life, attitudes, behavior?

10. Take ten minutes in the next week simply to be in God's presence without anything specific to pray about. Just be *with* him! Take note of what happens and how you feel.

Compare

11. Consider Matthew 6:8. Why is it good to tell God everything even though he knows everything before we tell him? What does it do for us when we tell God, and what does it do for God when we talk to him about something he already knows about?

12. Read Deuteronomy 6:4-9. Compare this passage, which has to do with teaching children the commandments, with Hallesby's statements about praying all through the day.

13. Hallesby states that there is more to prayer than asking. Read Ecclesiastes 5:1-3 to gain further insight into listening to God.

Think

14. Psalm 40:3 says, "He put a new song in my mouth, a song of praise to our God." Psalm 100:4 says, "Enter his gates with thanksgiving and his courts with praise." Is thanking and praising God a command to follow, something that should be entirely spontaneous, or both? Why or why not?

15. What might be some of the positive and negative outcomes of reciting the Lord's Prayer every day?

9

Problems of Prayer

Review

Hallesby cites five problems of prayer. Let's review each of them by stating the positive answers to the problems.

1. Much can be accomplished in prayer when helpless people in faith give Jesus access to their needs.
2. We should pray because it is through prayer that we begin the process of understanding and receiving all that Jesus desires to give to us.
3. God has made himself voluntarily dependent upon our prayer to accomplish what he desires through his church.
4. God has a plan for the world and his kingdom. The prayers of his children influence the means and methods, not the ends.
5. Though God has not pledged to answer the prayers of those who are not his children, he may choose to do so out of his love for them.

Examine

1. Why is prayer a question of the will and not a question of power?
2. Why is understanding God's character, especially the characteristic of love, essential to resolving questions related to problems in prayer?
3. What is the role of our intercessory prayers in bringing about God's work?

Apply

4. Of the five questions set forth by Hallesby, which one can you most identify with in terms of your own expe-

rience? Has this chapter helped to resolve any of your questions or problems? If so, how?

5. Do you have any questions or problems related to prayer that Hallesby did not address? Is there anything in this chapter, or the book thus far, that can help to clarify and answer your problem?

6. Attempt to be more aware of problems or questions you have regarding prayer in the week to come. If you have a prayer notebook, consider keeping a list of those questions or problems.

Compare

7. Hallesby states, "Our prayers are effective when we are strong in faith" (p. 151). James 5:16 states, "The prayer of a righteous man is powerful and effective." Look up the word "righteous." Is being righteous also a part of being helpless? How?

8. Hallesby also states, "In prayer the Church has received power to rule the world" (p. 158). Read Ephesians 1:15-23. How can the church rule, and how, through prayer, does the church receive the power to rule?

Think

9. Read Luke 11:1-13. In this passage a disciple asks Jesus, on behalf of all the disciples, to teach them to pray. When is it common for people to have questions or problems in prayer? If a person never has a question or problem in prayer, would this represent a problem in and of itself? Why or why not?

10

The School of Prayer

Review

God calls us to continuing education, especially when it comes to prayer. The central things the Spirit focuses on in his classes are, first, to reveal Christ to the believer every day. Second, the Spirit works at making us earnestly solicitous and genuinely concerned about others. Third, the Spirit teaches us the necessity of self-denial in connection with prayer.

Examine

1. Hallesby begins with the question: "Now do you dare to pray, 'Lord, teach me to pray'?" (p. 161). Why might he have used the word "dare"?
2. What do you think Hallesby's response would be to the following statement? All Christians are automatically enrolled in the school of prayer.
3. Read Luke 18:1-8. How does this passage express the main point of this chapter?
4. According to Hallesby, the Spirit instructs those in the school of prayer with the intention of making them "earnestly solicitous." Look up the words "earnest" and "solicitous" in the dictionary. How do their definitions expand your understanding of what the Spirit does?
5. Why do you think that Hallesby refers to intercessory prayer as "the finest" and "most exacting" work we can perform?

Apply

6. Have you ever prayed, "Lord, teach me to pray"? If not, what, if anything, would be keeping you from praying that prayer? Consider praying it soon.

7. If you have started a prayer journal, keep a list of the things you continue to learn about prayer. Share what you are learning with a Christian friend.

8. Have you ever wanted to take credit for answered prayer because you have prayed about a concern that was answered? What does Hallesby say about this attitude and behavior? Make a personal commitment about how you will and will not talk about the things you pray about.

9. Choose one of the following ideas in order to help you yield to the Spirit, the teacher in the school of prayer, on a daily basis.
   - Each morning pray a prayer of invitation to the Spirit to come and teach you more about prayer that day.
   - Memorize Ephesians 6:18 or Romans 8:26-27.
   - Spend time reading some of the following passages to gain a broader understanding of who the Holy Spirit is and what he does: John 14:15-27, 16:5-16; Romans 8:1-39; 1 Corinthians 12:1-31; Galatians 5:13-26; Ephesians 1:3-14.

Compare

10. Hallesby mentions that the Spirit teaches us the necessity of self-denial in connection with prayer. Examine the following passages and reflect upon the self-denial evidenced in the lives of people who prayed: 2 Samuel 12:1-23; Nehemiah 1:1-11; Mark 1:35.

11. Intercessory prayer is an important aspect of this chapter. Read John 17 to see how Jesus prayed for himself, his disciples, and all believers.

Think

12. You have now completed ten of the eleven chapters of Hallesby's book. Before you read and study the last chapter, what have been the most important new un-

derstandings of prayer you have thus far acquired? How have they affected your prayer life?

11

The Spirit of Prayer

Review

In this final chapter Hallesby briefly reviews each of the previous chapters and encourages the reader to pray to the Spirit, in childlike faith, about the issues presented in those chapters. The unifying theme is honesty and openness with the Spirit, who is ready to help us at all times and in all ways as we continue in the school of prayer.

Examine

1. Hallesby encourages us to leave our children a legacy in the form of our prayers for them. Now, "our children" can certainly mean our physical children, but it could also be appropriate to leave our community or church a legacy of our prayers. What would be the benefits, for you and for your children, of leaving this legacy?

Apply

2. Identify those whom you want to leave a legacy of prayer. Write their names in your prayer journal or on a piece of paper you can keep tucked in your Bible.

Compare

3. Prayer, as defined by Hallesby, is opening the door of our heart to Jesus in an attitude of helplessness and faith. Read a story of Jesus and his disciples in John 1:35-39. How would you apply this story to learning more about prayer?

Think

4. What will you do now that you have completed the book and study guide? Will you read the book again? Will you

read another book on prayer? Or will you simply begin to make a conscious effort to put into practice what you have learned? Whatever you decide, remember that we are all called to enroll in the school of prayer, which is always in session. And, remember that the Spirit of prayer loves you and longs for you to come to him so that he can teach you how to pray. May all of your life and prayers glorify the name of God!